BATTLE · FOR · BRITA

WARGAME THE
ROMAN INVASION
AD43–84

PETER DENNIS
with easy rules by **Andy Callan**

Helion & Company Limited

26 Willow Road, Solihull, West Midlands B91 1UE, England

Telephone 0121 705 3393 • Fax 0121 711 4075 • Email: info@helion.co.uk • Website: www.helion.co.uk

Twitter: @helionbooks • Visit our blog http://blog.helion.co.uk/

Published by Helion & Company 2017

Designed and typeset by Farr out Publications, Wokingham, Berkshire

Cover designed by Paul Hewitt, Battlefield Design (www.battlefield-design.co.uk)

Printed in the UK by Henry Ling Limited, Dorchester, Dorset

Text © Peter Dennis and Andy Callan 2016

Pictures © Peter Dennis 2016

ISBN 978-1-911512-03-5

British Library Cataloguing-in-Publication Data.

A catalogue record for this book is available from the British Library.

For details of other military history titles published by Helion & Company Limited contact the above address, or visit our website: http://www.helion.co.uk.

We always welcome receiving book proposals from prospective authors.

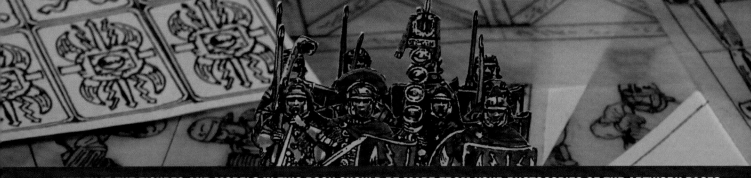

MAKING PAPER ARMIES

BEFORE YOU BEGIN

We call this series 'sourcebooks' because in them you can source all the artwork you will need to make armies of any size by making your own prints from the pages.

In the 18th and 19th century the publishers, like the famous Imagerie d'Epinal in France, sold paper soldiers by the sheet. Today, excellent colour copies can be made cheaply on commercial copiers, although just how cheaply can vary depending on your location. You can make copies on your computer at home, but I prefer to use a commercial copier, the print quality is better and the difference in price is worth it.

When you begin making copies of the soldiers in the book, take the staples out and cut the pages into single sheets for convenience. Store them in an A4 folder.

PAPER

The thickness of paper is expressed in weight terms. The standard copier paper is 80 gram, which is fine for making soldiers, but if you get serious about it, buy some good quality 100 gram paper. The surface of the paper makes a real difference to print quality and a bit of extra substance in the ranks is welcome. Don't be tempted to go much thicker for the soldier stands. Heavier paper is harder to cut out and the model has a more pronounced edge which works against the illusion that we are trying to create.

Commercial copiers will allow you to use your own paper and may discount the prints if you ask them nicely. I use 120 gram paper for trees and 160 gram for buildings.

You will need to find stiffer card for stand bases. If you can't find anything suitable lying around, a sheet of mounting board from a craft shop isn't too expensive and will base a large army. It's easy to cut with scissors, and the colour is irrelevant so buy the cheapest!

GLUE

Paperboys, which is what we call these soldiers, work because of glue. When you stick two sheets of thin paper together with a solvent glue like UHU or a white

PVA glue the result is a surprisingly stiff and stable laminate. It is easy to cut out when fully dry but keeps its shape well. I prefer UHU for the main task of gluing the stands of figures, but PVA, which can be painted on, has no smell and dries very stiff. Its inherent wetness does mean the figures, particularly larger ones like cavalry, dry with a curve in them, but once straightened the curve doesn't return. PVA is particularly useful for the final stage of construction which is a brush lick over the back of finished weapons like spears and swords. The glue dries invisibly and makes vulnerable model parts like the Legionary pila, their thin javelins, really strong. It only takes a moment and I now regard this as an essential process. I really notice the difference in older stands made before I discovered 'the lick'.

I use impact adhesive, the 'general purpose' type you can buy in every supermarket, for gluing the bases and for fixing on the front ranks. It has lots of 'grab' and makes the whole job much easier.

SCORING AND CUTTING

Scoring is gently cutting partway through a sheet of paper with a craft knife to give a crisp fold. It is an essential part of all paper modelling. I use an older blade, which makes the pressure less critical. I run the blade along the score lines on the figure sheets by eye. It is easier to see the blade/line contact point that way and it is much quicker. I use a ruler for scoring buildings or the centre line of trees.

It is probably the cutting out which looks most daunting, but it is pretty straightforward if you have the right scissors and technique.

There are many types of scissors which are suitable. I use various pairs, pointed, like the ones on the back cover and no bigger than around 6 cm from the nut. One of my favourites cost about a pound from a supermarket kitchenware department. You may well have suitable ones around the house.

The secret is to keep the cutting hand still and rested, and to move the piece being cut around. So long as you can

see the line you are cutting, and this is almost always the case, it is easy. Don't try to rush, ever. Your speed will naturally increase as your muscles get used to the fine movements required. I timed myself recently and I cut out a three rank stand in about four minutes without making any effort to hurry.

Cutting out with a craft knife is much slower, and harder work. If you are left handed you might be tempted to do this, but get a pair of appropriate left handed scissors from a dedicated lefty website.

If you snip off a spear or sword, *and you can find it*, just use impact glue to stick it to the back of the figure. The resulting weapon will be a few mm shorter, but in the horde nobody will ever notice. Paper is very forgiving.

All the front ranks are separate. This is so that it is easy to cut up between their legs. As soon as I began to experiment with this I saw that the improvement in the appearance of the stands was so obvious that it was well worth the little extra time it takes. There is base colour between their legs on the sheet, so the process is optional. A 'locator strip' is folded up where the front rank will stand.

A word on edges: there is a school, notably in Eastern Europe, of soldier makers who leave a fine white line around the figures. This probably evolved to strengthen the figure and I suppose it can look pretty smart, but it isn't necessary and in fact a perfect white line around the figures is hard to achieve. Paperboys were designed to be a moving illustration, so I'm not a fan of the halo.

A WORD ON WOAD

The Britons were famously tattooed and painted with the blue vegetable pigment called woad. I have not given the figures any decoration, as such markings tend to camouflage the 3D effect I'm trying to get, and in any case I'm not sure how well you would see them at this scale. Don't let this stop you from applying your own scrolls and stripes to the men if you wish. This is best done to individuals after they are copied and still lie in sheet form.

MAKING A STAND

There is a short film of me doing all this on Youtube. 'Peter Dennis Paper soldiers' should find it. You can link into it from the Helion website too.

Score carefully along the horizontal fold lines on your copy of the page. Accurate scoring should ensure a good match between front and back when they are finished. Cut out the individual stand strips. I make Paperboys two sheets at a sitting normally, so I do these processes six strips at a time.

Fold along the score lines so that the ranks and the locator strip stand up and the ground sits flat. Make sure the sides of the strip line up. Check the line-up of command strip standards etc. by cutting a spear tip on both sides and matching them before gluing. Glue generously the inside of each rank and the locator strip and close it. Keep a tissue handy for the glue that might leak out of the sandwich.

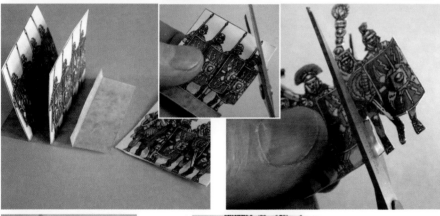

When the glue is thoroughly dry, fold the stand so that a rank is presented conveniently for cutting. Remember to keep your scissor hand still and move the stand around. Always cut from the front, and take your time! Trim the locator strip into an uneven arc. The cavalry locator should suggest a dust cloud. Cut out between the legs of the front ranks.

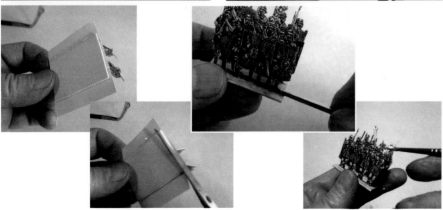

Glue your base card and centre it under the stand base. Trim the edges and glue the spare 'grass' underneath front and rear. Glue the front rank's feet to the front of the locator strip with impact adhesive. The final, very important step is to take a moment to brush some PVA glue onto the back of all projecting arms and weapons. This dries invisibly and will strengthen them a lot.

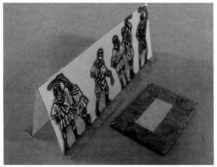

LIGHT INFANTRY, CHARIOTS, ELEPHANTS AND SCORPIONS

This is the first book in the series to feature open order infantry stands. If you have made the artillery in earlier books in the series, these are made in the same way. These instructions also apply to Scorpion crews.

Score, cut out and fold the figure strips with the narrow base grass folded outwards, Glue the figures, but not the base. When the glue is dry, cut out the individuals and trim the 'grass' around their feet into a rounded shape.

Cut out the base squares and glue your card base centred on the back. Trim the corners, don't forget to allow for the base card thickness, and glue underneath. Glue the figures randomly to the base keeping them square with the front edge. Use 'general purpose' impact glue, the slight shine on the printed grass is not glue-friendly. Don't forget the lick of PVA on weapons.

CHARIOTS

Paperboys are designed with a strictly 'from the front' philosophy which presents problems when dealing with a deep and complicated item like a chariot. The German Zinnfiguren makers didn't worry about such things and would just have shown the vehicle from the side. Indeed, I'm currently doing the same with designs of transport like limbers and wagons for later periods, but when the thing has to stand in line of battle with infantry and cavalry, presenting the edge of a sheet of paper just doesn't look right. So this

model is a rendition of a chariot within the limitations of our FTF credo.

They are made as two elements, the horses and the vehicle. The base has two locator strips, and the cut out parts simply glue to them like normal front rank strips. The wheels of the chariot are thin and provide a rather delicate link to the ground, so there is a 'yoke pole' of doubled paper which fits between the chariot and the horse team's yoke. Glue this well with impact glue, and it will help to keep the chariot securely upright. It is rather fiddly to fit I'm afraid and tweezers will help.

ELEPHANTS

These are perfectly straightforward to make. Note that the crews are designed to be enveloped in the howdah (the box on the back of the beast) so make the crew first and incorporate them in the construction. I made the head separate so you can vary the look of your elephants. This allows a spacer, perhaps a scrap of base card, to fit between the head and the body, which helps the illusion of depth. Fold his ears back slightly to hide it.

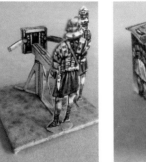

SCORPIONS

This weapon is presented in two styles. You can make a simple version, or a more complex one with more scores and folds. The pictures show the basic construction of the complex one, which is perfectly straightforward. There is also a carrying crew, inspired by a team of reenactors who manhandled their unit artillery alongside the legionaries. The Romans deployed quite a lot of these, and the artwork is presented twice in the book.

TESTUDO

The Testudo is just a box. If you lightly score and slightly curve the shield lines on the 'roof' before you glue it together you will help the illusion. Glue it to a stiff paper base.

THE ISLANDERS

The people that the Roman invaders encountered when they landed in Britain were very similar to the Gauls they had conquered in Caesar's time. They were divided into many tribes with all the alliances and quarrels you might expect. There was no overall ruler of Britain and the Romans were able to employ the 'divide and conquer' strategy familiar to colonialists through the centuries. Some tribal leaders were already familiar with the comforts and benefits of the 'Roman peace' in Gaul and were willing to ally themselves with this new and muscular force on the scene against troublesome neighbours.

Others however were not, and tribal alliances formed to resist the forced entry of Rome. Post invasion, rebellions sprang up to shake off the irksome yoke of the alien, notably under the famous warrior Queen Boudicca.

The armies which the Britons put into the field were naturally similar to those the Romans had encountered fighting the Gauls. Their military effort was the male population of the tribe fighting to defend their own land and they had no formal army like the Romans. They were, however, practised in war by their inter-tribal fights and were familiar with the ground they fought on and its potential for ambush. Massive earthen hill-forts were their last refuge, but the prospect, looking down on the professional preparations of the Romans must have been a grim one.

The main British tactic was the sudden charge of the warrior band. With their large shields and long celtic swords they presented the Romans with an enthusiastic challenge, particularly if they managed to appear unexpectedly. The Romans were equipped to resist such attacks though, and if they manage to hold the first impulsive onslaught, they could expect to prevail.

The younger men of the tribe would serve as missile troops, and the archaeological evidence represented by stores of pebbles suggest that the sling was a primary weapon. Cheap and effective even against armoured targets, the sling should not be under-rated. Clouds of light armed youngsters would plague the formations of Romans, keeping them under a constant clatter of stones, any of which might strike a helmeted head with fatal results.

Horses were important to the tribesmen and Celtic cavalry was respected, and often recruited, by the Romans. They could operate as light cavalry, showering an opponent with javelins as they gallop past, or form up and charge. Despite the lack of stirrups at this time the supportive saddles allowed a considerable impact.

Chariots had disappeared from the Roman world's battlefields, but not in Britain. Caesar reported that his men were intimidated by the performance of the British charioteers during his earlier brief invasion, and we might imagine that Claudius' soldiers were too. They were the preserve of the wealthier members of the tribe, and appear to have been used either as battle transport to bring elite infantry into action or as a rapidly mobile platform for missile fire. I imagine that army commanders would be chariot borne unless they wish to fight among the ranks at some crucial point.

Morale, as ever, was a crucial factor in the struggle. The mysterious Druidical religion of the Britons does not seem to have been a creed of peace and love. We might expect that commanders would fire up their men, if they could, with the Druids' incantations. What we do know is that the Romans hated the Druids and went to some lengths to wipe them out.

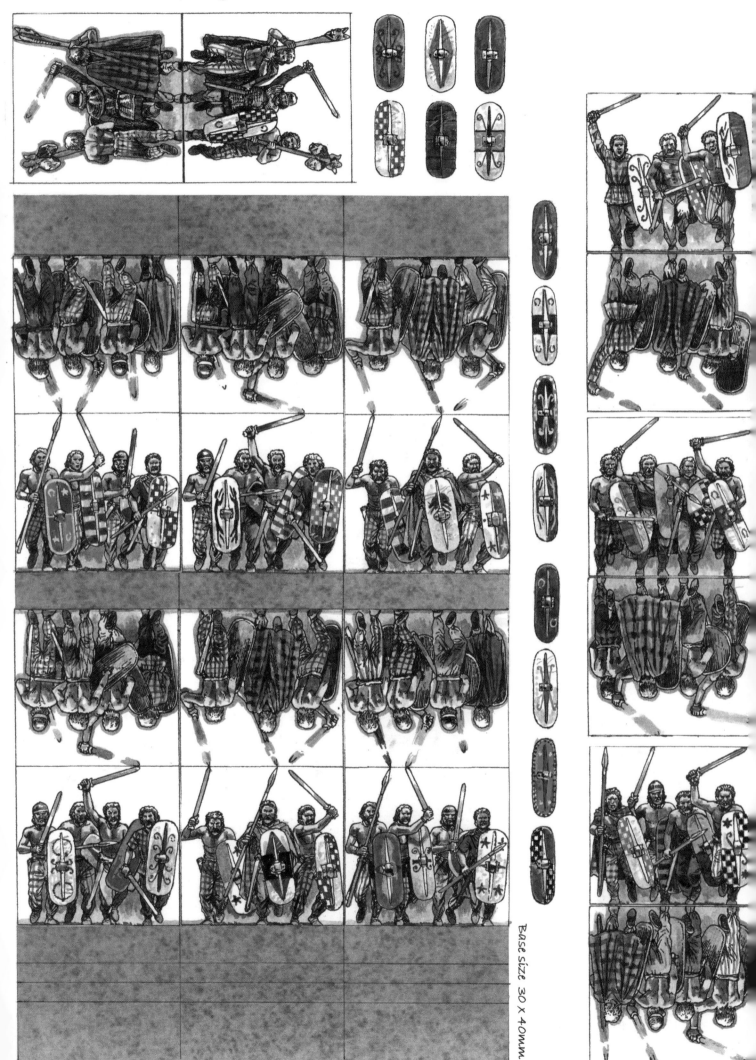

Base size 30 x 40mm

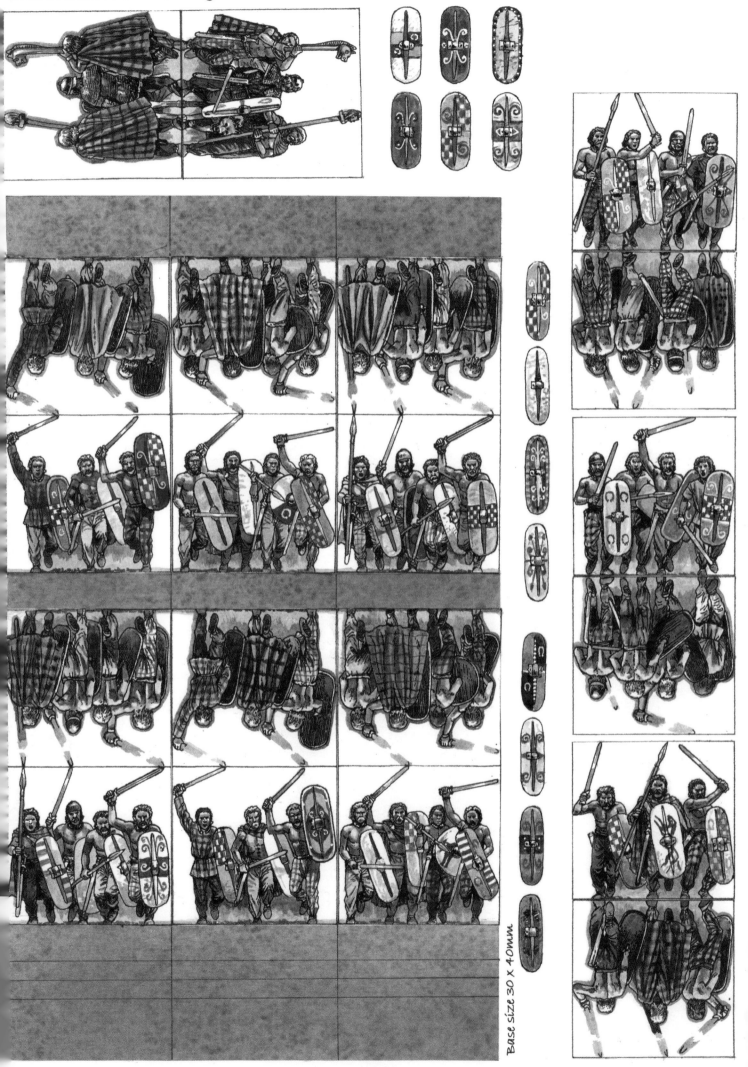

Base size 30 x 40mm

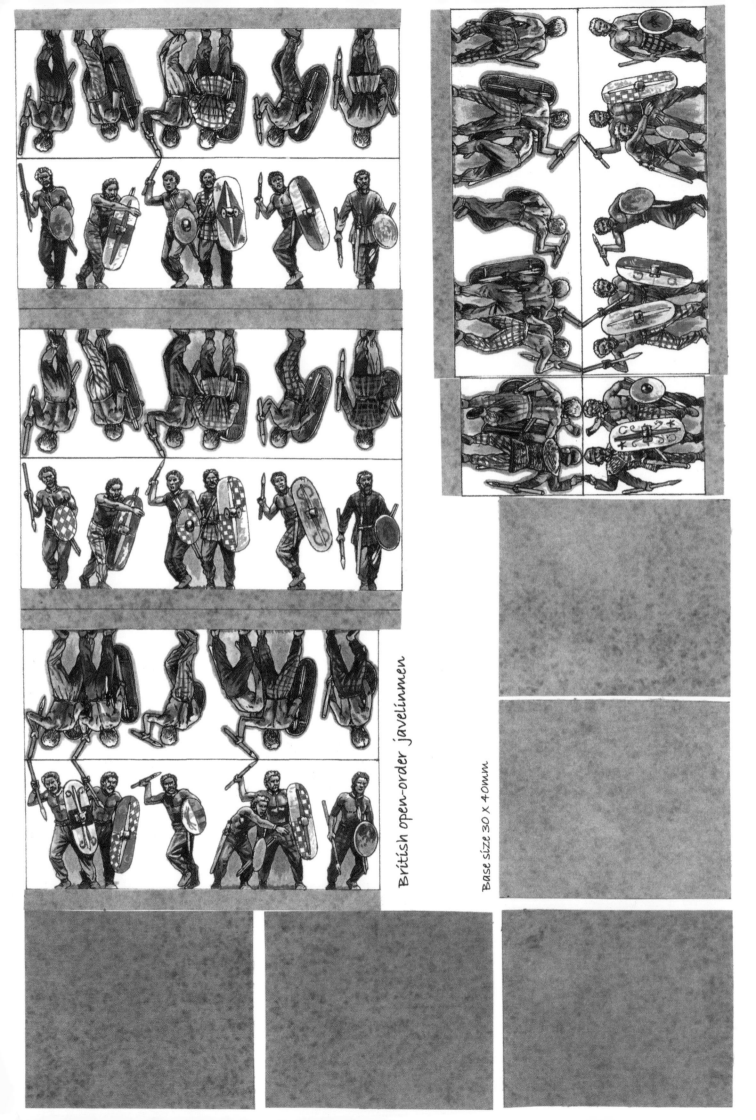

British open-order javelinmen

Base size 30 x 40mm

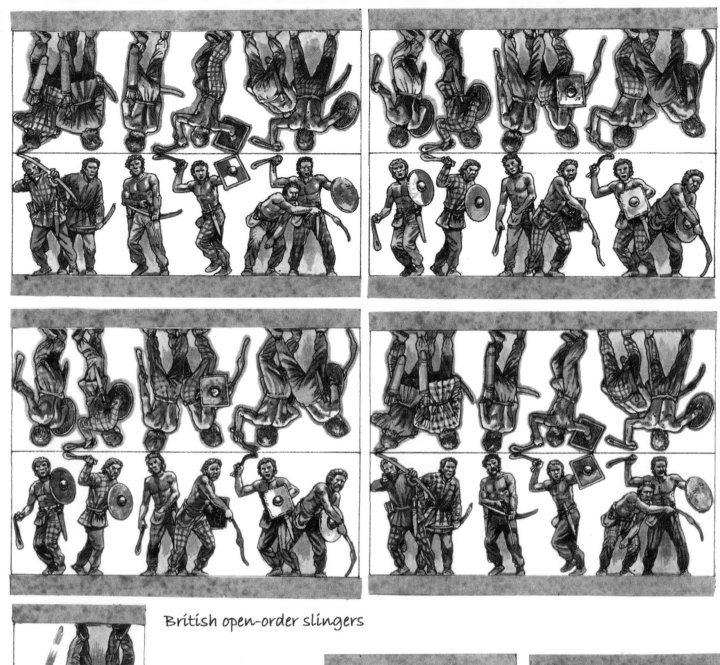

British open-order slingers

Base size 30 x 40mm

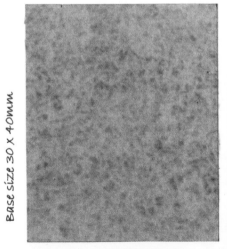

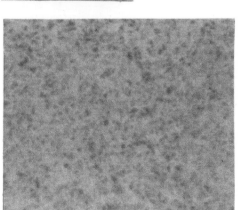
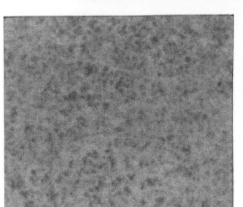
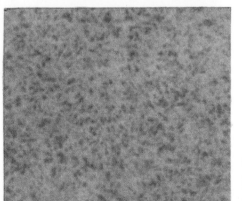

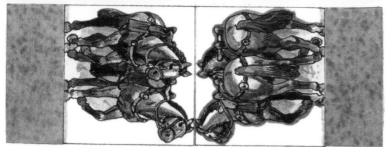

Cavalry casualty

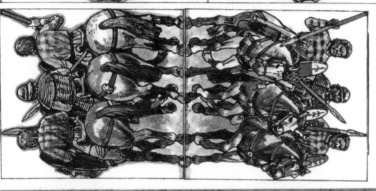

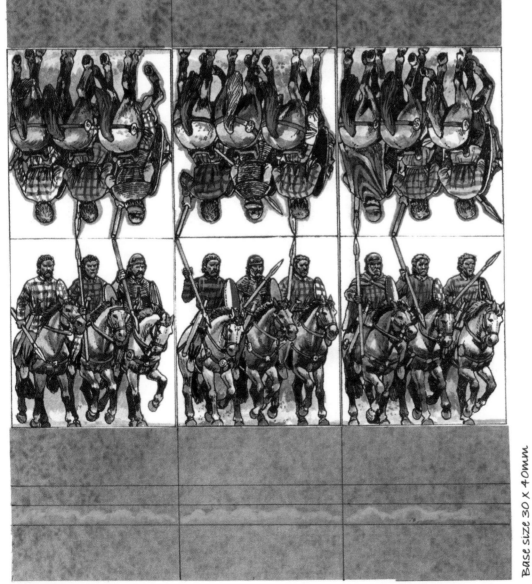

Base size 30 x 40mm

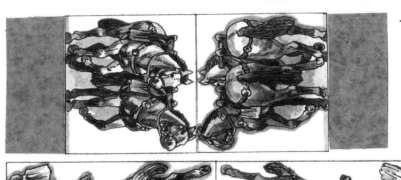

British open-order cavalry

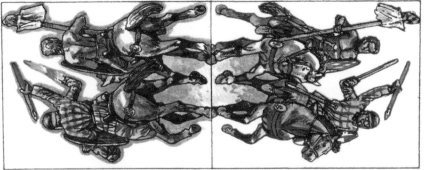

Cavalry casualty

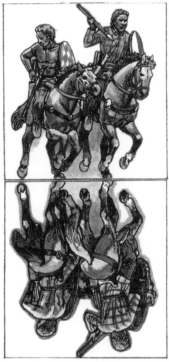

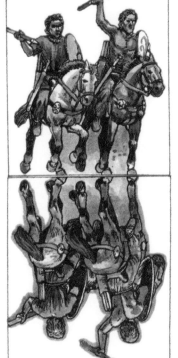

Base size 30 x 40mm

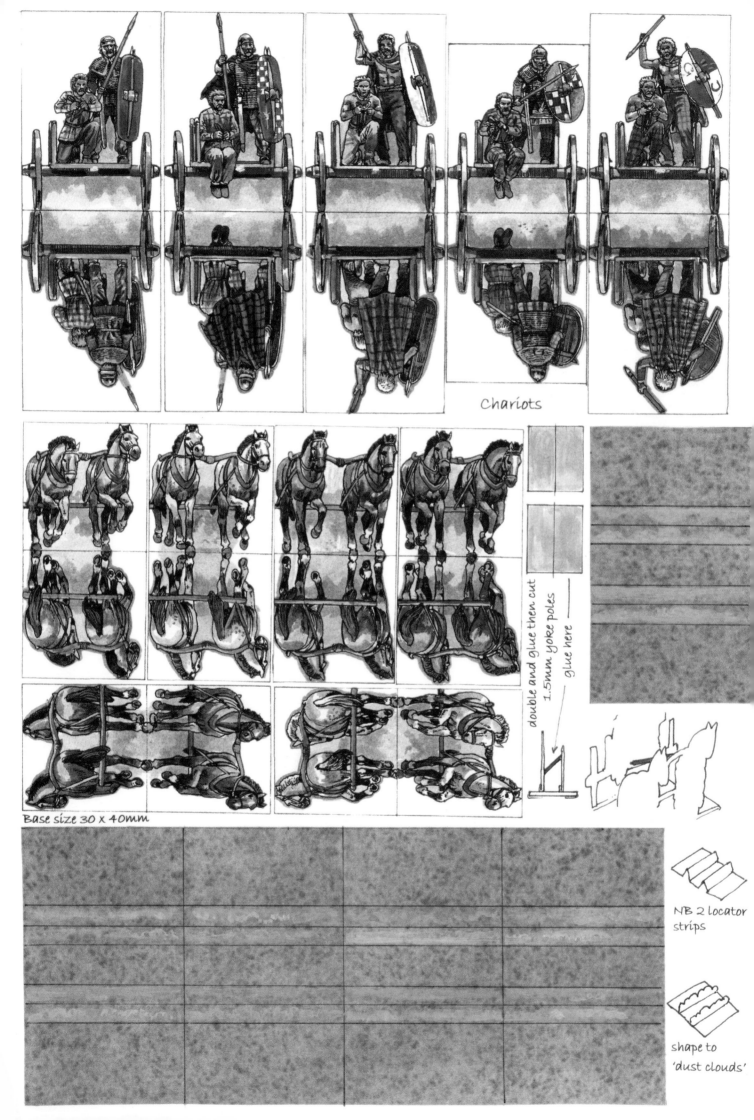

Chariots

double and glue then cut
1.5mm yoke poles
glue here

Base size 30 x 40mm

NB 2 locator strips

shape to 'dust clouds'

British commanders

Sacred grove ritual items

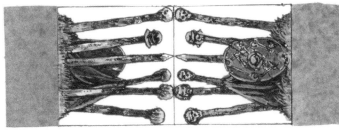

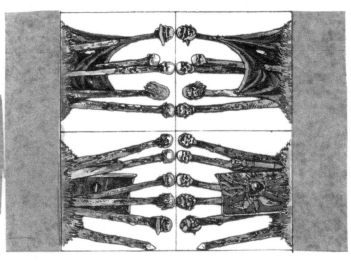

Foot commander strips

Boudicca

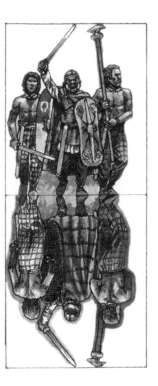

Druids

Base width 15mm

Boudicca

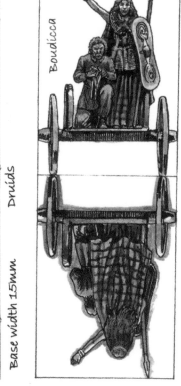

THE ROMAN ARMY

By the time Claudius launched his invasion fleet onto the shores of Southern Britain the Roman Army had conquered a vast empire around the Mediterranean Sea and modern France, at that time called Gaul.

The four legions he sent to Britain were institutions of military prowess, all established for well over a hundred years. They were the second Legion Augusta, the ninth Legion Hispana, the fourteenth Legion Gemina and the twentieth Legion Valeria Victrix. The legionary soldiers dedicated their lives to the army, enlisting for 25 years.

THE INFANTRY

The Legions numbered around five thousand infantrymen at full strength and were the armoured core of the army. They were divided into numbered cohorts of around five hundred men, which our game uses as the basic tactical unit. They wore full body armour and carried the pilum, a heavy javelin with a long iron shank designed to pierce shields and the deadly gladius, a short sword for close work in the melee.

Alongside them were auxiliary infantry recruited from conquered nations who might be fielded in roughly equal numbers. They were armed with an oval shield and a spear rather than the pilum. Auxiliaries were tough fighters but were expected to do the military donkey work in a campaign, too. Some units had special skills. The Batavians, from modern Holland, for example were called on to swim the Danube in one campaign. Others might be javelin-throwing open-order skirmishers.

Specialist missile troops were recruited from regions where that weapon was skilfully employed. Composite bowmen were recruited from the Middle East, and slingers from the Balearic Islands, for example. Cast lead slingshot that whistled alarmingly in flight added to the effect of their weapon.

A light bolt throwing catapult called a 'scorpion' was available to every infantry unit. Accurate and hard-hitting, it could reach out and sting the enemy beyond the range of bows and slings.

THE CAVALRY

'Roman' cavalry was all recruited from the best of the mounted troops of conquered nations. They served in uniform and in established units called 'Ala' as auxiliaries and were considered to be at least the equal of any cavalry they might meet in Britain.

ALLIES

British tribes whose leaders were sympathetic to the invaders could be persuaded to accompany the Romans in the field. The Romans were always keen to divide enemy nations in this way. Native cavalry and infantry might scout for the main army, or even join in the battle to overpower rival tribes. One can imagine the bitterness that must have been engendered amongst their countrymen by such alliances.

MODELLING THE ROMANS

There are optional front ranks for the Legionaries, which can be made with pila, like the back ranks, or shown with drawn swords. Be careful with the legionaries, as well as the irregular troops and Britons, not to have matching front and middle ranks so a naturalistic look to the units can be achieved. Command and standard strips are on a separate sheet and should be given to one stand in six instead of a front rank as the cohort commander, if you are using Andy's rules.

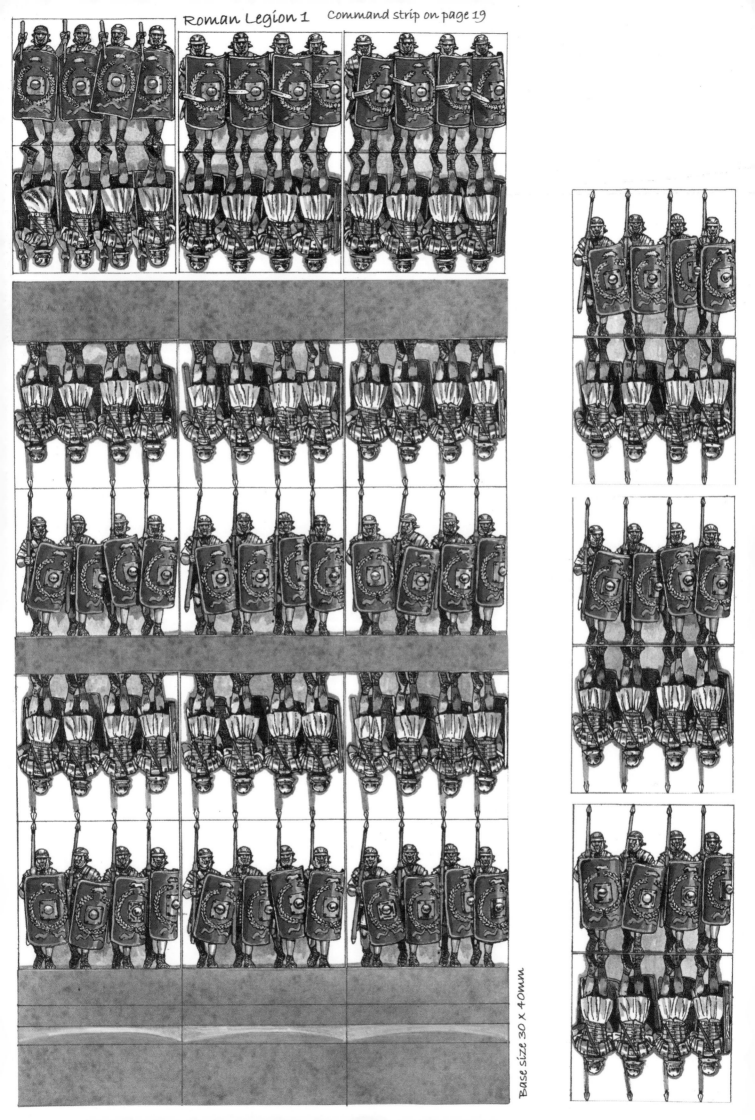

Base size 30 x 40mm

Roman legion 2

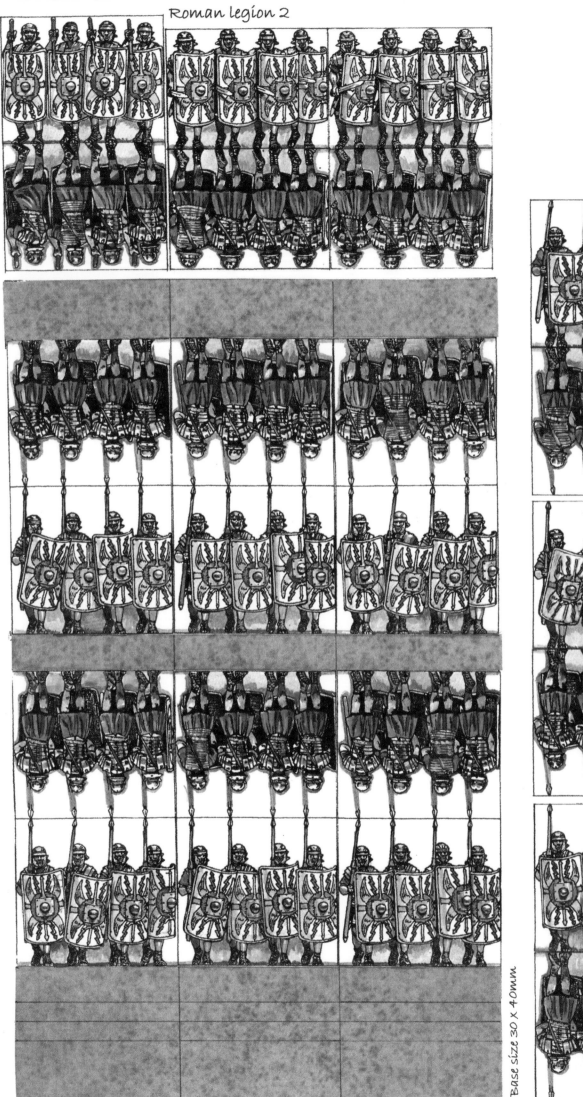

Base size 30 x 40mm

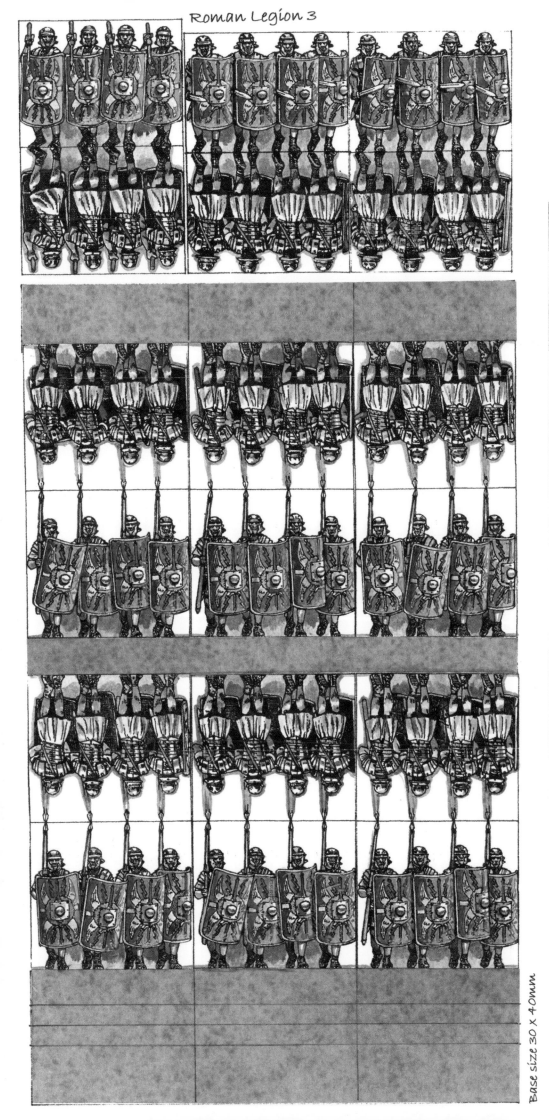

Base size 30 x 40mm

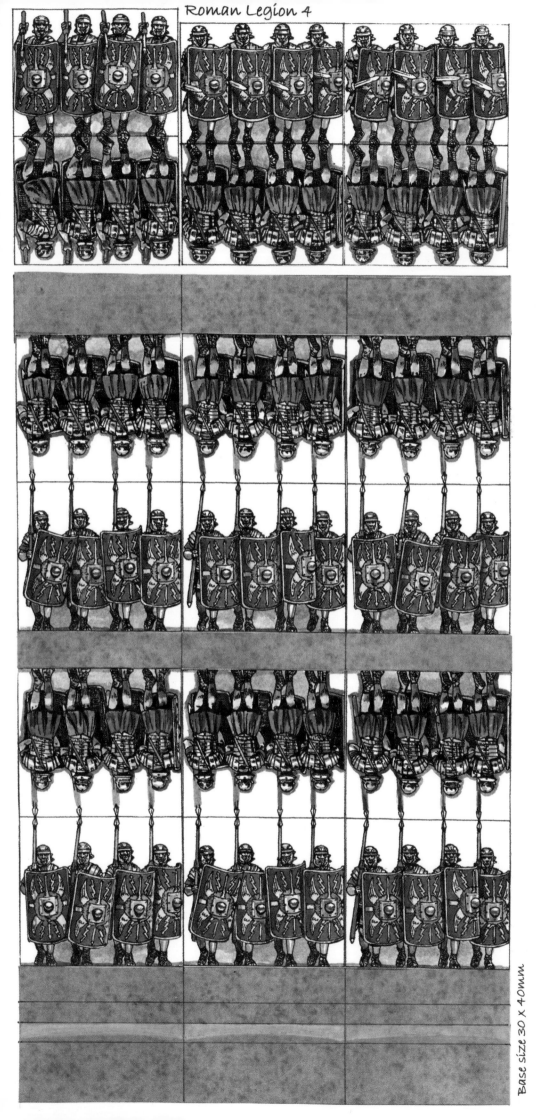

Base size 30 x 40mm

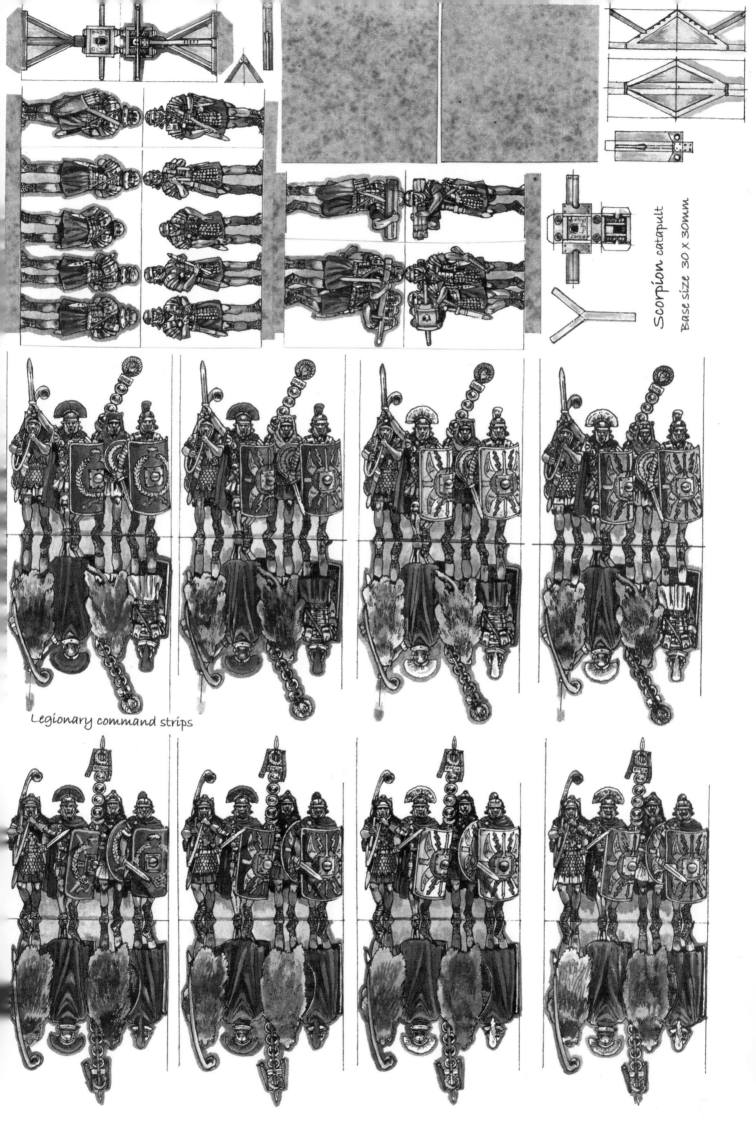

Scorpion catapult
Base size 30 x 30mm

Legionary command strips

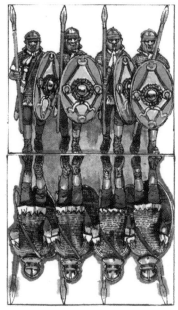

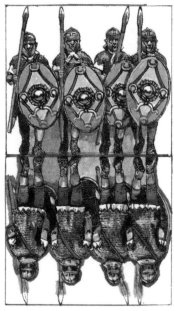

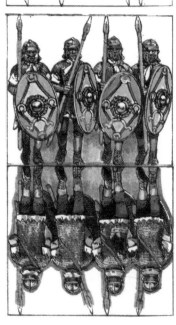

Base size 30 x 40mm

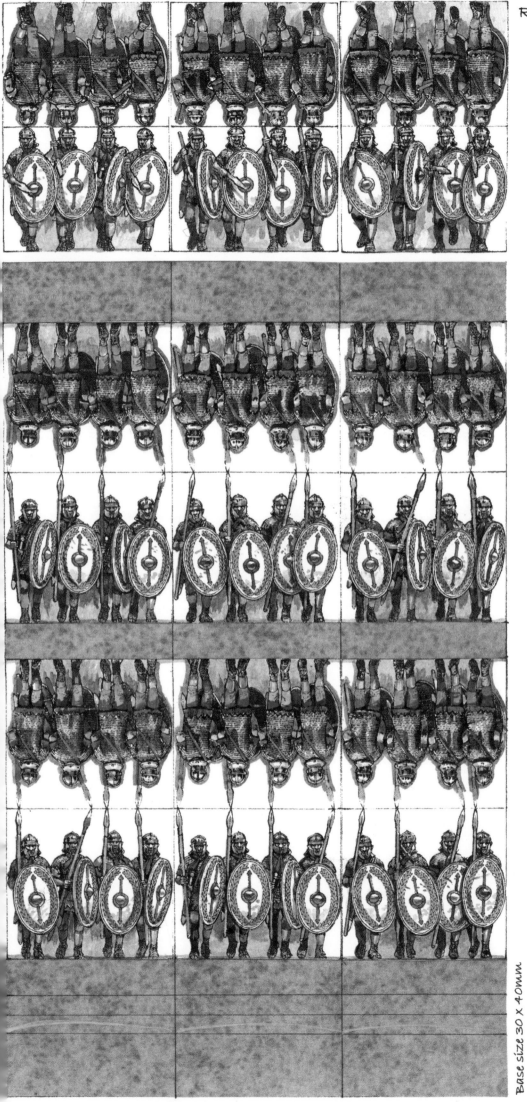
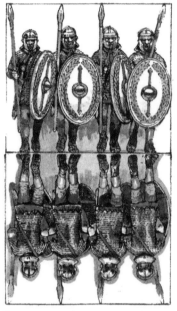
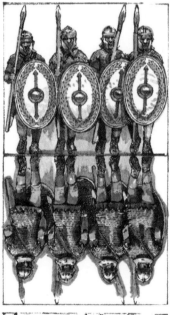
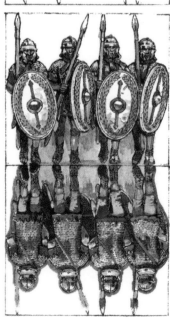

Base size 30 x 40mm

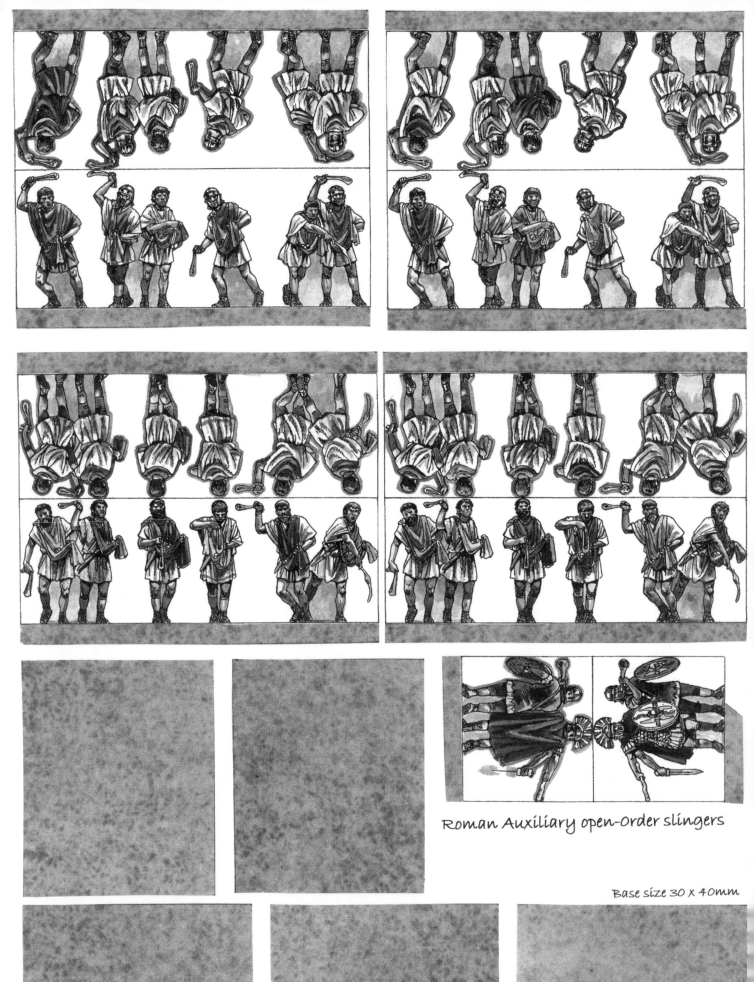

Roman Auxiliary open-Order slingers

Base size 30 x 40mm

Roman Auxiliary open-order javelinmen

Base size 30 x 40mm

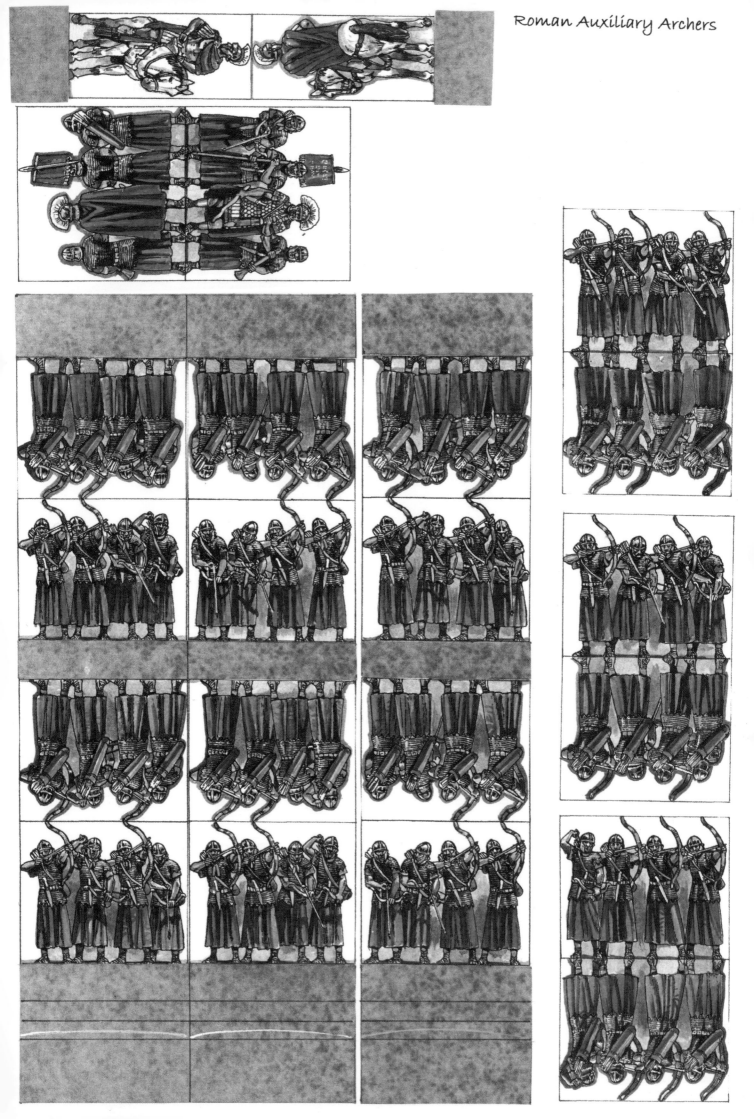

Roman Auxiliary Archers

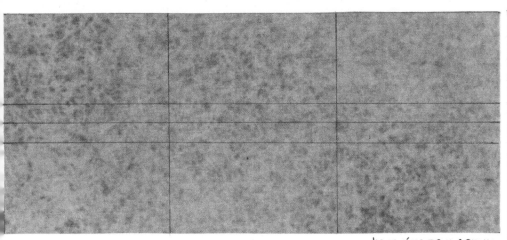

base size 30 x 40mm

War Elephants

Enfold crew in howdah →

Glue thick card spacer between head and body →

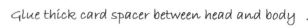

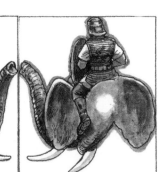

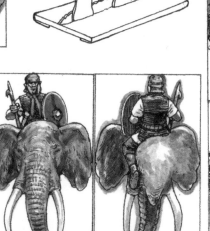

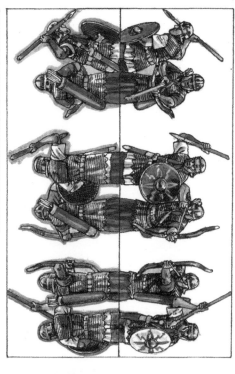

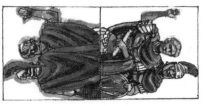

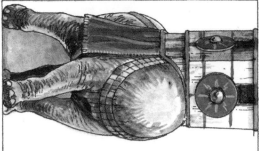

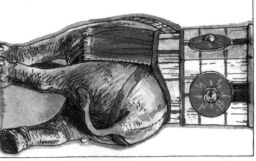

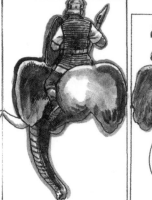

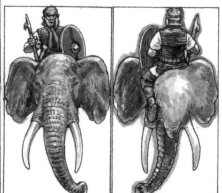

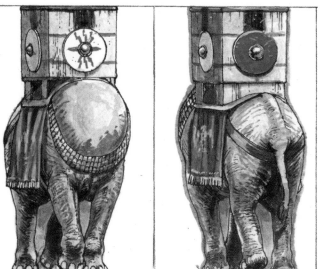

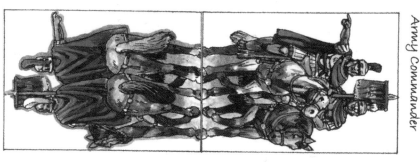

Roman Commanders

Auxiliary command strips

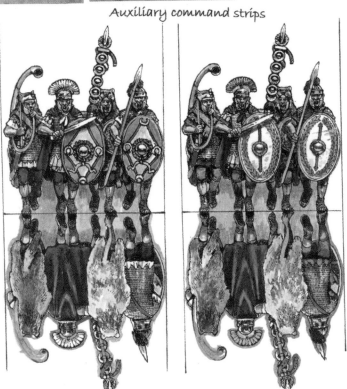

Legion Eagle standard party. Glue as front rank with a command strip and a legionary strip behind. One per Legion.

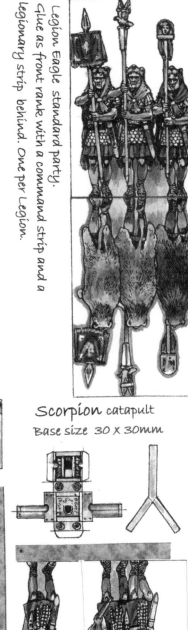

Scorpion catapult

Base size 30 x 30mm

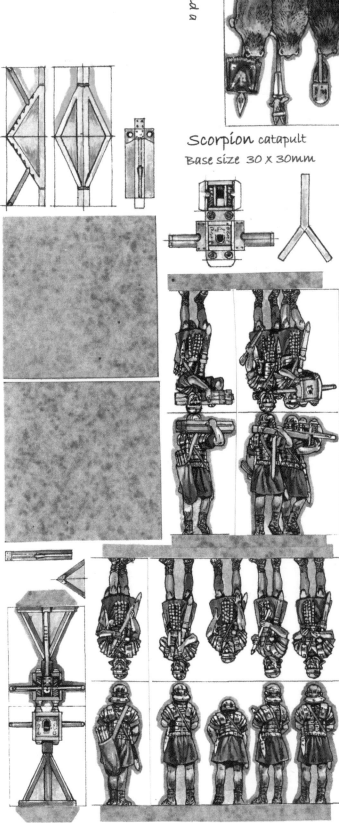

Testudo

Make as a box. Use stiff scrap paper for the bottom. Lightly score down the lines of shields on the 'roof' and add a little curve to each line round a pencil. This will help the illusion!

casualties, both sides

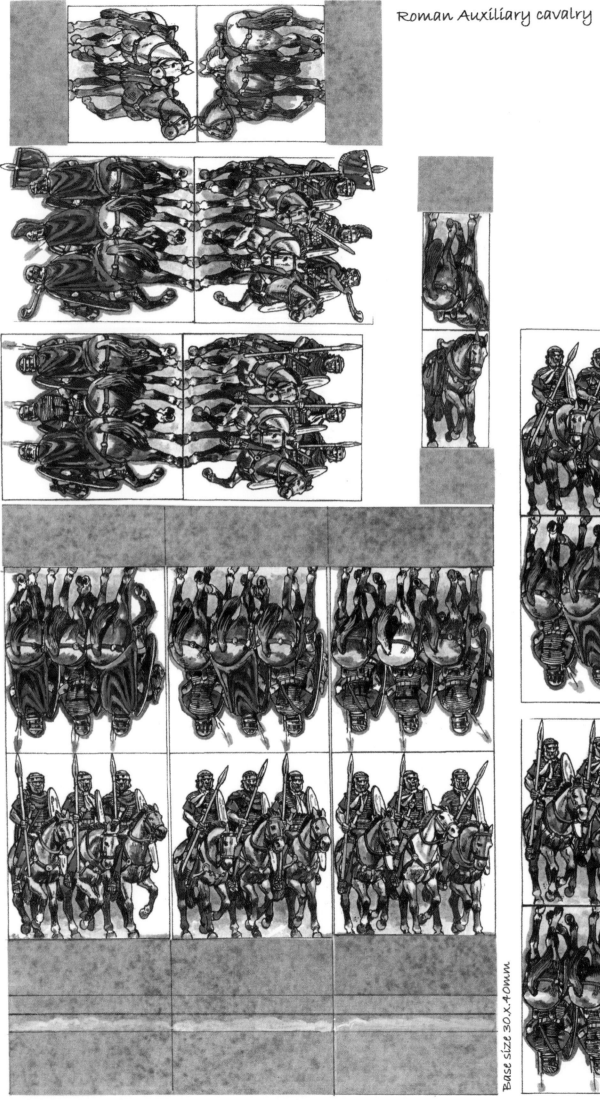

Roman Auxiliary cavalry

Base size 30.x.40mm

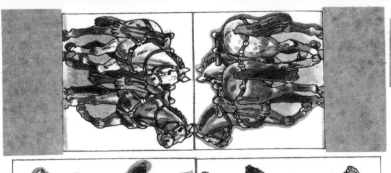

Roman Auxiliary open-order cavalry

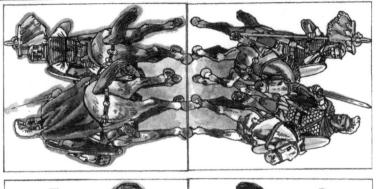

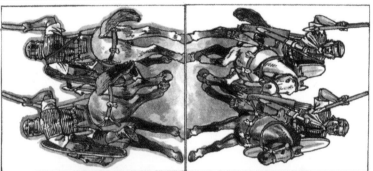

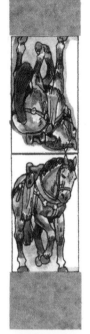

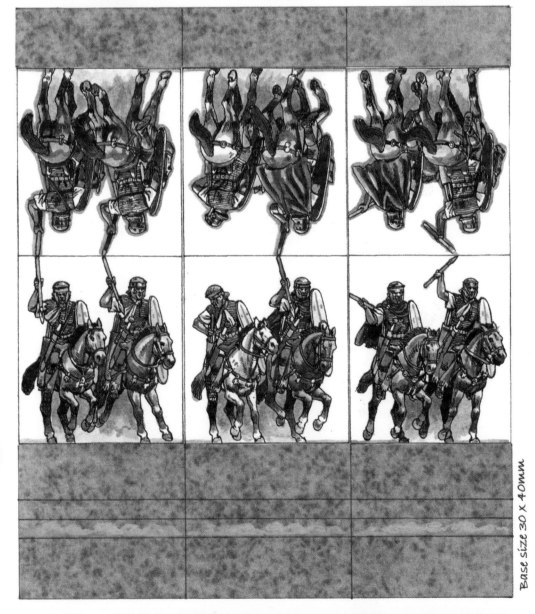

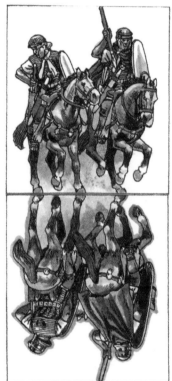

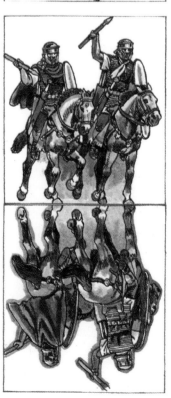

Base size 30 x 40mm.

MAKING THE BATTLEFIELD

The light weight of paper soldiers makes them ideal for use on the traditional wargame terrain, a ground-coloured cloth laid over book hills, their contours softened with newspapers. You could dye an old sheet, which would be in the Paperboys spirit of inexpensive wargaming, or look at the products of several companies which make specially printed sheets for this purpose. The base colour of the troops in this book is the 'open grassland' pattern which Cigar Box Battles has kindly allowed me to copy from their sheet of the same name.

THE MARCHING FORT

I have added tiny sketches to the terrain model pages to help new paper modellers. I have tried to make a convincing 'marching fort' of the sort the Romans would dig every evening to secure their camp ground. They carried the wooden stakes with them to make their ditch and bank more formidable. The stakes could be tied into a 'cheval de frise' a spike horse, which I speculate could form a gateway obstacle.

Print the sheets onto heavy paper if you can, or reinforce the base with card if not. The earth-coloured base strips of the spikes can be opened out flat to face the front of the bank with their points, or opened less and used to glue the spikes as a fence along the bank ridge. I glue each corner to one 'bank' strip which makes them more stable.

THE BARGE

The troop carrier barge is based on ones on Trajan's column, being used as pontoons. I speculate they would be rowed by the troops themselves, so I didn't make a mast. It needs care to make. Make sure the base is glued to quite stiff card and is centred in the hull. It will seem too small at first, but the stem and stern posts are quite deep and should squeeze up to a good fit at either end. Once that assembly is glued and dry, drop the deck, which needs to be glued to postcard thickness

stuff, into position. It will seem like it won't fit at first, but gently open out the hull and persist and a snug fit should result. When you have fitted it, take it out and glue the deck support before returning it. The deck sides don't really need glue, but a post-build brush with PVA would seal them. You can mount a scorpion on the deck house if you trim the base slightly. Pure speculation on my part, of course.

TREES

Through the series I have built a tree collection, and for this one I couldn't resist a spooky set of ancient oaks for the Druids' sacred grove. Birches, the first trees to colonise open ground, are the other.

Score fold and glue the trees and bushes. cut them out as flats like the figure models. You will notice a thin centre line down the tree. Cut one of the flats cleanly in half down that line with a craft knife, or large scissors. Take two other flats and score that line on one side of each. Fold

down the score line to an angle of 60 degrees or so and glue the straight edge of a half-tree into the open score line. You will then have a 'three tree'. Glue the base circle to a coin and fold down the edges. Edge glue the base of the trunk to the base centre with a good blob of impact glue.

The brushwood entanglements are an innovation inspired by one of Andy's scenarios. Exploiting nature's tendency to obstruct was a technique used through the centuries to make a difficult barrier for the enemy.

ROADS

The post-invasion Roman roads on the back inside cover have a box running either side to show the raised pavement, which is optional. They need a stiff card base, or can be glued to thin MDF, folding down the edges to cover the thickness of the board.

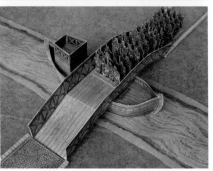

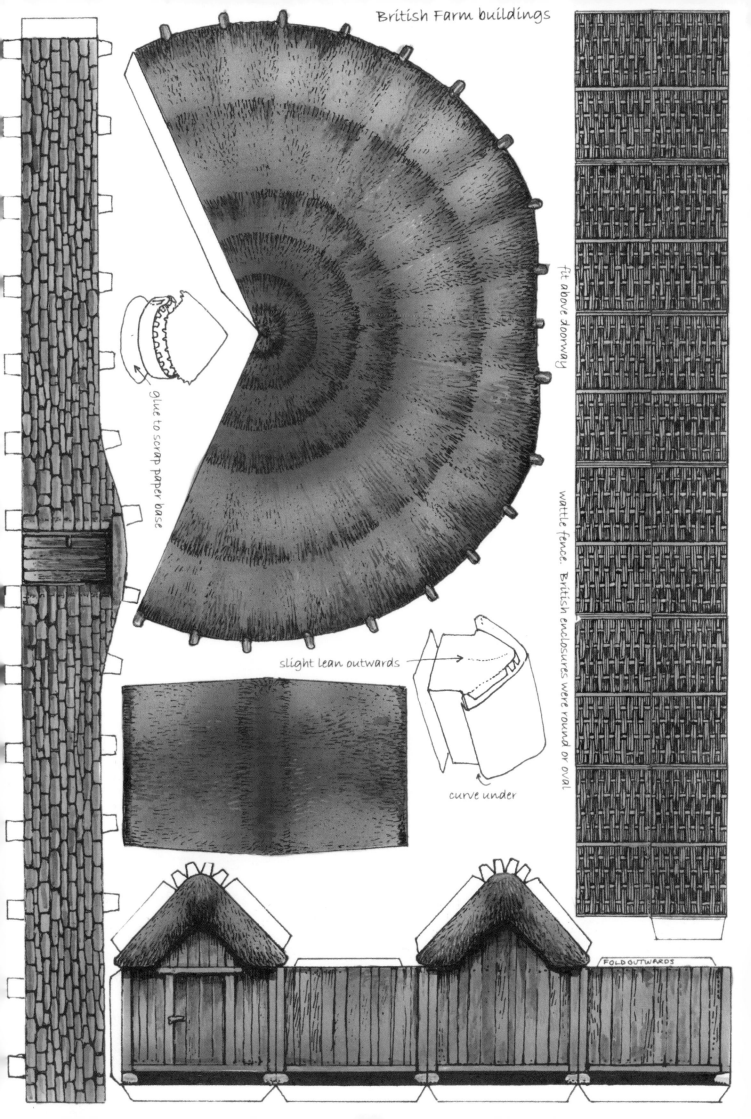

British Farm buildings

fit above doorway

wattle fence. British enclosures were round or oval

glue to scrap paper base

slight lean outwards

curve under

FOLD OUTWARDS

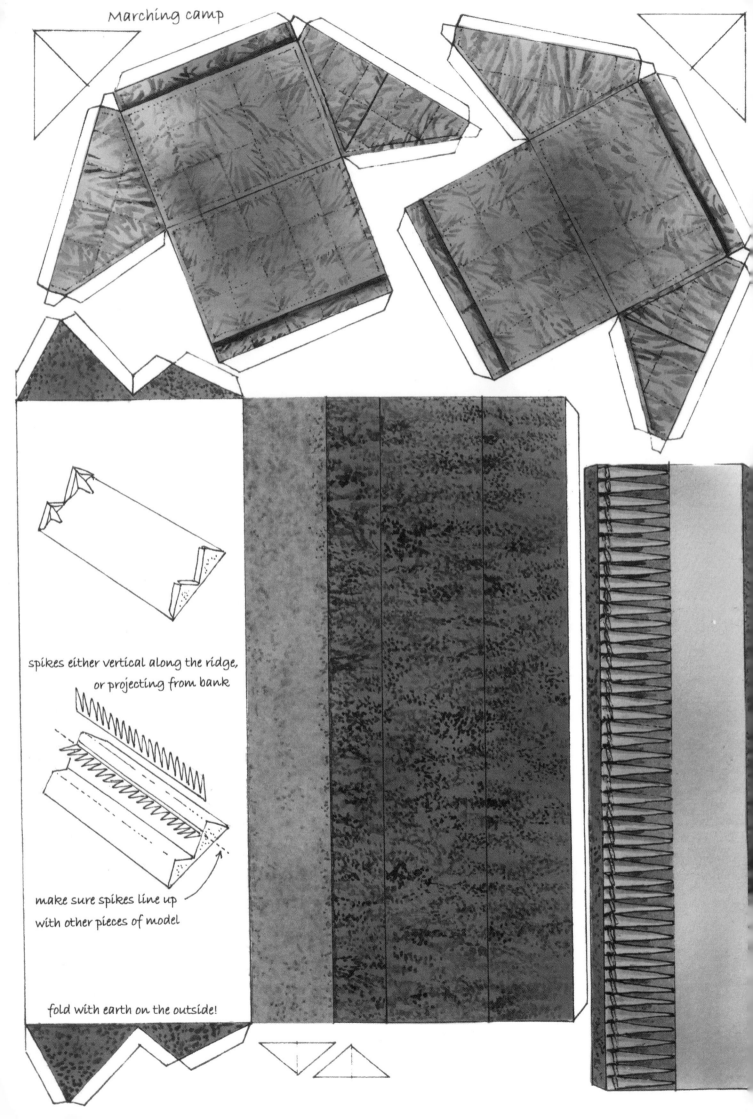

Marching camp

spikes either vertical along the ridge,
or projecting from bank

make sure spikes line up
with other pieces of model

fold with earth on the outside!

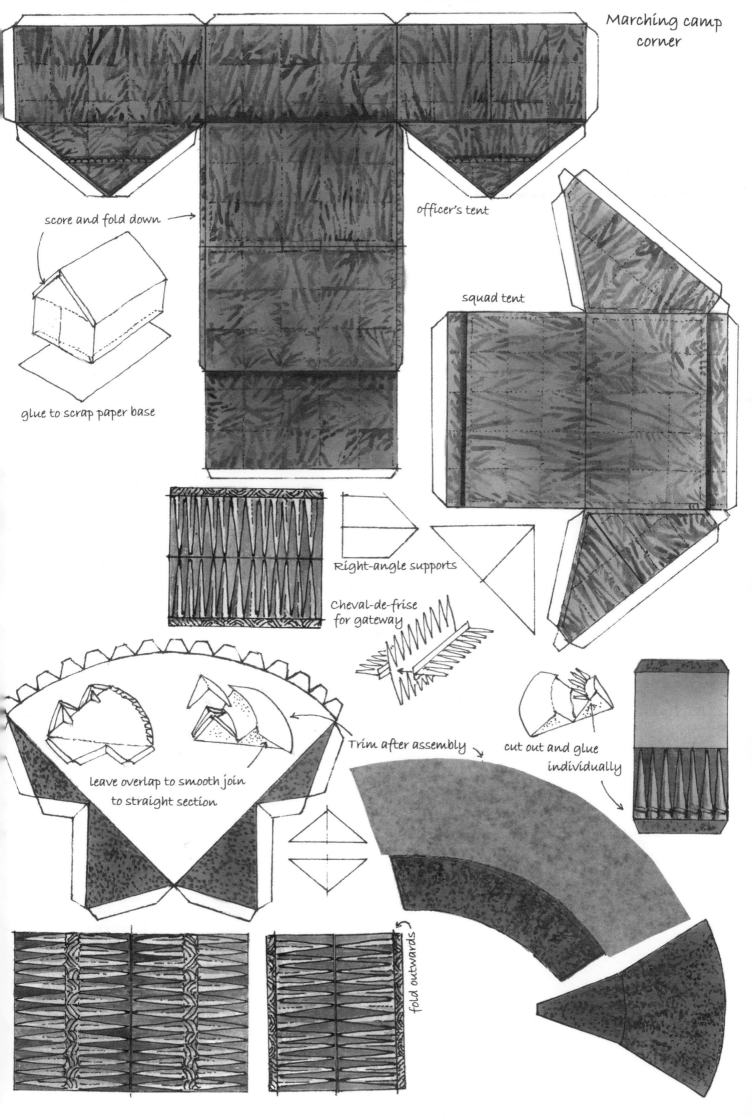

Marching camp corner

score and fold down

glue to scrap paper base

officer's tent

squad tent

Right-angle supports

Cheval-de-frise for gateway

leave overlap to smooth join to straight section

Trim after assembly

cut out and glue individually

fold outwards

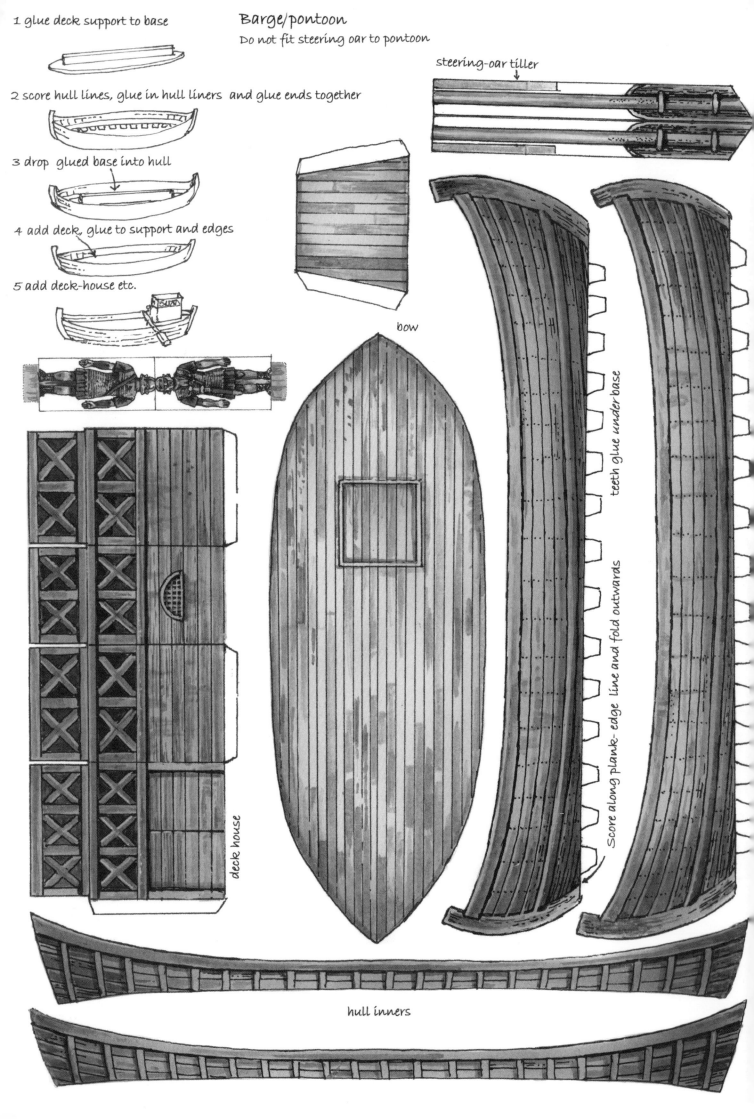

1 glue deck support to base

Barge/pontoon
Do not fit steering oar to pontoon

2 score hull lines, glue in hull liners and glue ends together

3 drop glued base into hull

4 add deck, glue to support and edges

5 add deck-house etc.

steering-oar tiller

bow

teeth glue under base

Score along plank-edge line and fold outwards

deck house

hull inners

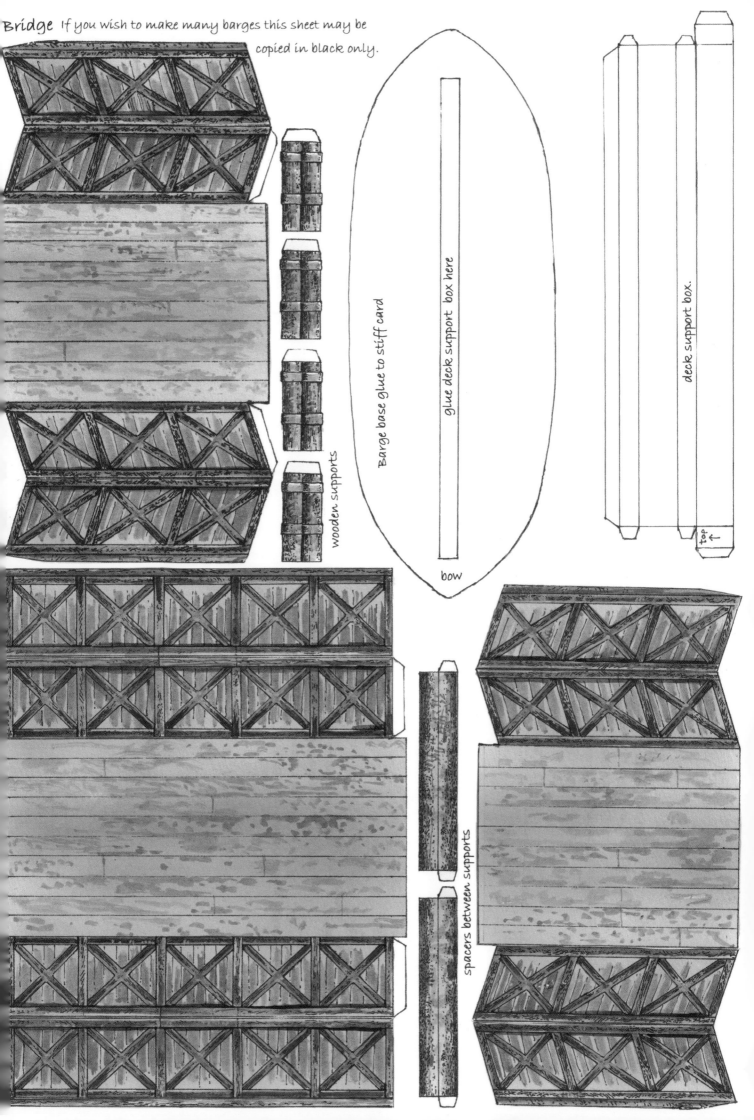

Bridge If you wish to make many barges this sheet may be copied in black only.

wooden supports

Barge base glue to stiff card

glue deck support box here

bow

deck support box.

top

spacers between supports

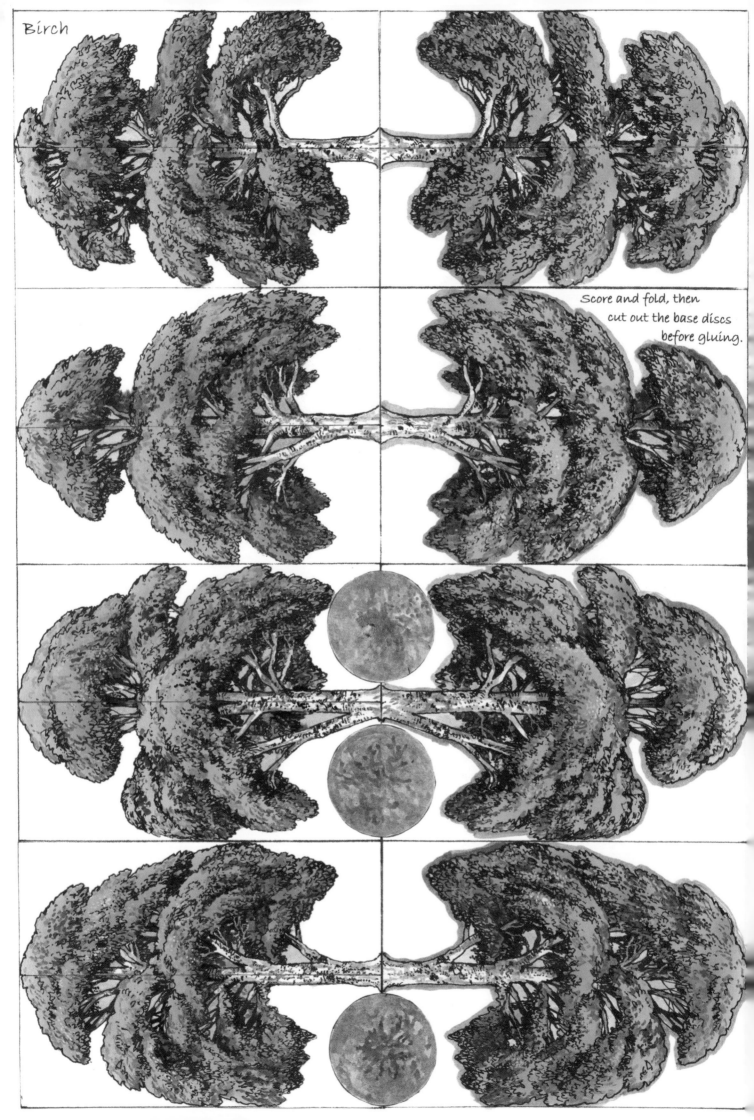

Birch

Score and fold, then
cut out the base discs
before gluing.

Sacred Grove oaks

Score and fold, then cut out the base discs before gluing.

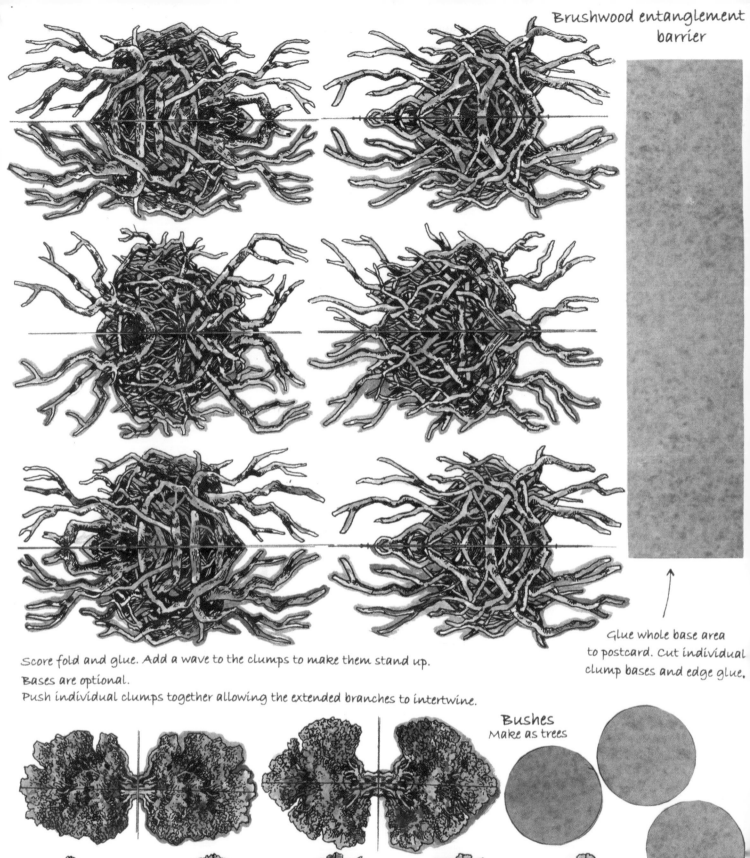

Brushwood entanglement barrier

Glue whole base area to postcard. Cut individual clump bases and edge glue.

Score fold and glue. Add a wave to the clumps to make them stand up.
Bases are optional.
Push individual clumps together allowing the extended branches to intertwine.

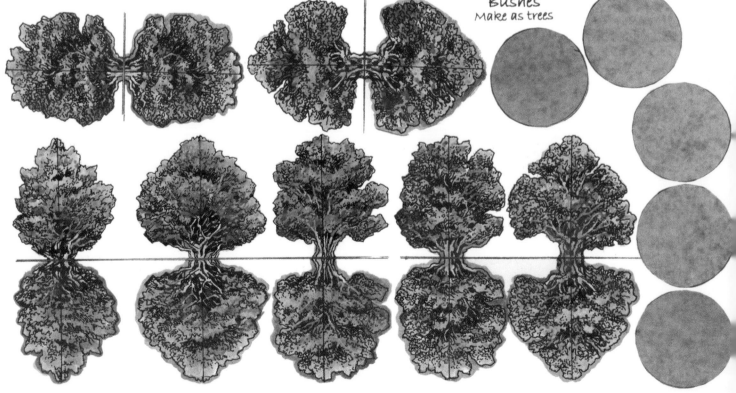

Bushes
Make as trees

WARGAMING WITH PAPER SOLDIERS

INTRODUCTION

These paper soldiers are suitable for use with any of the modern, published wargames rules which use multi-figure stands. In the older style rules individual figures were removed as casualties – this was still progress from the very earliest days of the hobby, a century ago, when figures were knocked over by matchsticks fired from toy cannons!

But in order to give our readers a full set-up in this one book, we are providing some relatively simple rules which we hope will get you up and fighting battles with our paper soldiers.

If you have never played a wargame before you should turn to our Beginners' game on pp47-48. This will introduce you to way the rules work. Play this a few times before moving on to the full version of the game (pp40-43)

More experienced wargamers may feel confident enough to go straight to the full version but we suggest that you still start with smallish actions involving about half a dozen units a side. Then, once you have got used to the command and combat mechanisms you can move on to bigger battles using the full range of different troop types.

What you need

Enough paper soldiers to make up two armies.

At least two players, one on each side – but the more players you have, the livelier the game.

A ruler or other measuring device and a handful of dice (the six-sided type or "D6") for each player.

A table to play on, the bigger the better.

Scale

At full strength, a Roman Cohort had 480 men, organised in 6 "centuries" of 80 men each (see the photograph, above). Clearly, it is not going to be practical to use this "1:1" scale in a game, so our units are reduced in scale while still trying giving an impression of what they are supposed to represent. The ancient authors gave some very implausible accounts of the size of "barbarian" armies, so we don't claim any consistent figure: man ratio for our troops.

Instead, we use "standard-sized" units as the basic building blocks of our armies. One of these standard units of Infantry or Cavalry consists of 6 stands.

British Warbands are less rigidly organised and come in different sizes – 6, 8 or 10 stands strong. Units of Elephants or Artillery (Roman Scorpions) are only 3 stands strong, but they may also be split up into single stands which operate attached to individual Infantry units. Chariots operate independently as single stands but may join a friendly unit in Combat.

These units do take up quite a lot of ground, so really big battles need a big space. A smaller action of around 10-12 units a side will still give two players a tactically challenging game but it will fit on a dining room table. In any case, this size of army is about as many units as one player can comfortably handle. Anything bigger will need more players and a larger playing surface.

Army Points

Some wargamers like exactly evenly matched sides and rules often provide detailed army lists and points values to allow them to do this. We generally prefer more informal methods to muster our armies but if you insist on equal points, here is a simple points system you can use for these rules:

Skirmishers and Slingers: 1 point per stand **Legionaries, Warband, Auxilia, Archers, Cavalry, Chariots, Elephants & Artillery:** 2 points per stand

We suggest British armies should always "out-point" Romans by at least 25% else the Romans' superior discipline will make things too one-sided. Players who are new to the game should always be given more points than experienced Players, to help even things up.

Choosing a battle

You can fight one of our example battles (see pp45-46), use the format suggested by our examples to design something similar yourself, or simply make one up from scratch. You don't need to stick to Romans vs Britons. Why not set up a battle from a Roman Civil War or British inter-tribal conflict?

Randomised Army Lists. This method will usually give the Britons a significant points advantage – they'll need it! Use a standard pack of playing cards (with Jokers). First agree on how many units you want in each army (depending on the number and variety of units you have available, of course) and then deal cards to each player, from a shuffled pack, one card per unit:

RED 2-9: a unit of Roman Legionary Infantry or a British Warband*
BLACK 2-9: a unit of Roman Auxilia or a British Warband*
Roll a dice for each British Warband:
5 or 6 = 10 stands strong, 3 or 4 = 8 stands, 1 or 2 = 6 stands.
Any 10/Jack: a unit of Roman Skirmishers (Open Order Auxiliary Javelinmen) or Slingers or Artillery (you choose): OR two units of British Slingers and/or Skirmishers (Open Order Javelinmen) (you choose)
Any Queen: a unit of Roman Light (Open Order) Cavalry, or 2 units of British Cavalry (1 Light – Open Order and 1 Heavy – Close Order)
Any King: a unit of Roman Heavy (Close Order) Cavalry or a Dice roll +3 British chariots
Any Ace: a unit of your choice AND draw an extra card from the pack. *A Roman army can never choose more than one unit of Elephants or Archers!*
Joker: Remove one of your opponent's cards, drawn "blind" from his hand.

Laying out the Armies

We decided against providing any rules for creating the terrain on the battlefield – that's up to you. Remember that Roman armies preferred open countryside on which to fight their battles while a wise British commander would try to have woods and other dead ground in which to hide troops in ambush. So you need to have a mixture of types of terrain to even things up.

For formal battles, ancient armies usually deployed with the Infantry in the centre and the Cavalry on the two wings, usually preceded by skirmishers and other missile troops.

WARGAMES RULES FOR ROMANS vs BRITONS by Andy Callan

"Luck made up for any deficiencies in his strategy…" (Tacitus)

The Basics

Army Organisation

Organise your Armies into "units". Most units of Infantry or Cavalry consist of 6 stands.

A unit moves and fights in a line 1 or 2 stands deep. Missile troops can only shoot their front rank.

British Warbands should be a mixture of 6-, 8- and 10-stand units. They always operate in a two stands deep formation - with an odd number of stands the extra stand goes in the front rank.

Artillery and Elephants operate in units of only 3 stands, or singly, attached to infantry units.

Chariots operate alone as independent stands. They may join a friendly unit for Combat.

A **Formed** unit has all its stands aligned and touching. Show a **Disordered** unit by staggering its stands.

Dice This game uses ordinary, 6-sided dice (D6). Halves always round DOWN.

Measurements.

Moves are in multiples of 8cm – two stands width, or roughly 3" imperial. Ranges are in multiples of 4cm. Use a tape measure or ruler or make a special "measuring stick" with these markings.

Measure movement from a front corner of a unit and range from the front edge of any shooting stands. Try not to quibble over exact measurements. An easy-going attitude and a bit of give and take here will make for a smoother-running game and more lasting friendships…

Setting up the Battle

Total up the number of points worth of troops in your army (see "Army Points"), make a note of it and declare it to your opponent.

Next, agree a "Breaking Point" for each army – a level of losses beyond which the army is at risk of a sudden collapse of Morale. One third losses is a good level for most games, but this can be set lower or higher depending on how much time you have available and how stubborn the players are. See "Victory and Defeat" (Phase 6, below) for how this works.

You need to keep a careful tally of any points lost as the battle progresses. Put any Destroyed, Panicked or Routed stands in a "dead pool".

In a standard, set-piece battle, the two armies should deploy at least 60cm apart.

The Turn sequence

Dice each turn for which side shoots first (Britons go first if the scores are tied) and again for who moves first (Romans go first on a tie).

There are **six distinct phases** in each turn. Note that it is important to follow this sequence exactly in each turn of the game:-

1. **Shooting**: First one side shoots any Artillery, Archers or Slingers it wants to, then the other side does the same.
2. **Movement**: First one side moves any units it wants to, then the other side does the same – but any units that are now in contact with the enemy can't move.
3. **Close Combat**: Any units in contact with an enemy must fight each other.
4. **Morale and Discipline**: Units might suffer a loss of **Morale** because of the casualties they have suffered in combat or from enemy shooting. They might also have to test their Discipline to see if they **Panic**, or if they **Pursue** a fleeing enemy.
5. **Rallying and Re-forming**: after becoming disordered.
6. **Victory and Defeat**: Check to see if the battle has been won or lost.

Phase 1: Shooting

Dice at the start of this phase to see which side shoots first – Britons win a tie.

1.1 Ranges and Targets

Artillery (Scorpions): Range = 32cm

Slings & Bows: Range = 24cm.

Javelins and Pila: Range = 8cm

The shooting Arc for all weapons is 45 degrees to either side of a stand's front corners. You can't shoot if there is a friendly stand less than 8cm away from your target.

Archers can shoot over the heads of a friendly infantry unit, if the target is over half Range.

Any Missile troops can shoot over the heads of friendly troops who are downhill of them

Troops normally either shoot OR move but any Slingers or Archers who choose to shoot at only half effect (by halving the number of shooting dice they roll) can then make a half move.

Note: *Hand-hurled Missiles used at very close range (javelins and pila) do their "shooting" during a different phase of the turn.(see 2.3 (e) and 3.1 ,below).*

1.2 Effects of Shooting

Artillery and Archers roll 2D6 per stand, Slingers roll 1D6 per stand.

Roll only half this number of dice if the target is Skirmishers, Slingers or Chariots. Targets in woods can't be shot at. Any 6s rolled are hits. Then make "Saving Throws" for any hits.

1.3 Saving Throws

Roll 1D6 for each hit on a unit (+1 in fortifications or Legionaries in Testudo)

Roman Legionaries: save for 3/4/5/6 - on a roll of 1 or 2 the stand is destroyed

Roman Auxilia and Heavy Cavalry: save for 4/5/6

Roman Archers, Skirmishers, Artillery and Light Cavalry: save for 5/6

Elephants are a special case: see 3.4

British Chariots and Heavy Cavalry: save for 4/5/6

British Warbands save for 4 ½ /5 /6 (for any 4s roll again – save for 4/5/6 on this second roll)
British Skirmishers, Slingers and Light Cavalry: save for 5/6

1.4 Which stands are destroyed?
Roll another D6. On an even number count that many stands from the right of a unit and remove that stand. For any further losses keep counting in the same direction, circling back if necessary. On an odd number count from the left.

Phase 2: Movement
Dice at the start of this phase to see which side moves first. Romans win a tie.

Begin by doing any compulsory moves (retreats, routs and pursuits – see 4, below) first and test for any potential Panics (see 4.2) that arise as a result of such moves.

2.1 Orders
If a unit starts its move more than 32cm from the nearest enemy it will always carry out its orders. Any closer and you must test to see what happens. First say what you want the unit to do and then your opponent rolls a dice. Different troops react in different ways.

Romans (all types of troops)
Any roll of 1 means the unit moves only half distance, or if ordered to carry out a special manoeuvre (see 2.3) it stands still instead (*maybe they ran into an unseen obstacle or they mistook the order*).

For a Group of Roman units (each separated by no more than 8cm) who are all given the same order (e.g., "All take ground to the right") roll only one orders dice for the whole group.

British

Warbands and Heavy Cavalry: are "Aggressive" troops who always enthusiastically obey an order to advance towards the nearest visible enemy, so they don't need to roll, in such cases.

For any other order (including an order to "stand still" or "re-group"), roll a dice for each unit.

Any roll of 1or 2 means that the unit disobeys and instead it makes a spontaneous rush at the nearest Romans in sight, continuing to advance until it can attack in close combat. The only time this doesn't apply is if the Britons concerned are hidden in ambush, or if the nearest Romans are Skirmishers (and so not worthy of being attacked).

Light Cavalry, Skirmishers & Slingers: any 1 means they fail to move or carry out a manoeuvre.

British Chariots: never have to roll for orders – they act independently on their own initiative.

2.2 Move Distances
- Heavy Infantry (Legionaries, Warbands and Archers): 16cm, Warbands can charge 24cm.
- Light Infantry (Auxilia, Skirmishers and Slingers): 24cm
- Cavalry & Chariots: 32cm, Heavy Cavalry can charge 40cm.
- Artillery can be manhandled 8cm or pivot to face any direction.
- Elephants: 16cm.

All units may advance in a straight line directly forward or diagonally forward up to 45 degrees to the right or left of their front corners. Infantry can also back off half a move.

2.3 Special Moves and Manoeuvres
  a) **Wheeling and Turning**
     Legionaries, Warbands & Elephants can wheel up to 90°, pivoting on one corner, and not move, or up to 45° and then move half distance.

     Auxilia and Cavalry can wheel up to 90° and then move OR vice-versa.

     Skirmishers and Chariots can wheel in any way, move normally and then wheel again.

     All troops except Chariots and Skirmishers take half a move to about face.

  b) **Taking Ground** is done by edging sideways – by no more than half a normal move.

  c) **Re-Grouping**
     Roman units can change their formation in any way (e.g., to go from a 2 deep line to a 1 deep line, or to close any gaps caused by losses)on the spot, so long as all stands in the unit end up touching. They can then move only half distance in that turn.

     British units can re-arrange D6 x stands in a unit and then move up to half distance. Treat this as their "orders" roll, so a 1 means they fail to re-group and they must advance against the enemy instead, in their current formation.

  d) **Passing through a friendly unit**
     Romans can pass through any friendly, stationary unit.
     British skirmishers, slingers, cavalry or chariots can pass through each other freely. Otherwise, move one unit up to touch the other and roll 4/5/6 to successfully pass through. On a roll of 1/2/3 both units are disordered for the rest of the turn.

  e) **Moving and throwing javelins**
     Light Cavalry, **Chariots** and **Skirmishers** can throw their javelins at any time in the movement phase - before, during or after their move. Roll 1D6 per stand, hitting for 6 Equivalent enemy units and Missile troops must then make saving throws. Against other troops See 3.1 (below) for the effect of such shooting.

Crossing a linear obstacle: (ditch or stream) will temporarily disorder Legionaries and Warbands and any Mounted troops for the rest of the turn – they halt on the other side. The same thing applies to fortifications, but Mounted troops can't ever cross them.

Woods and Broken Ground: all Roman troops move at half speed (they are very wary of being ambushed!). All Romans except Skirmishers and Auxiliaries are disordered in combat in woods.

2.4 Attacking and Charging
Any advance that brings you into contact with the enemy becomes an "Attack".

Skirmishers can only attack other Skirmishers or Missile troops. Missile troops never attack.

A Charge is an Attack made at charge speed. Only Heavy Cavalry and Warbands can charge.

A Charging unit must move straight ahead, without any wheeling and the enemy must be at least half a charge move away. A Warband can charge only once in a battle, a Cavalry unit can charge twice.

No troops can charge up a hill with steep slopes, across an obstacle or against fortifications.

6. Phase 3: Close Combat
3.1 Preliminaries
Cavalry moving second may always **counter-attack** enemy cavalry (ie meet attacking or charging enemy Cavalry half way), but enemy cavalry who moved first and charged will have an advantage in combat (see 3.2 below).

Evading an attack is something Skirmishers, Slingers, Cavalry and Chariots can always try to do - they turn and get an immediate free half move (disordered) away from the attack.

Roman Legionaries throw their pila just before combat. Roll a dice for every front rank stand the first time a unit throws pila, hitting for 6. Then roll only half the dice the second time. Roman Auxilia throw javelins, rolling dice for half the front rank in the 1st & 2nd round. Hit for 6.

Any hits inflicted during this phase by **Pila** and **Javelins** will do damage to the enemy formation but cannot destroy any of his stands – so you don't make any saving throws. An attacking stand that takes a hit in this way will not close with the enemy and stops 4cm (1 base depth) short, instead. A defending stand that takes a hit backs off 4cm. In either case this creates a gap in the line which will reduce the number of "fighting stands" eligible to roll a Combat dice (see 3.2).

Lining up Try to align the opposing stands so that they are in full contact with each other even if the attack has come in at an angle – be prepared for a bit of give and take here and this will save a lot of arguments about who can fight whom.

3.2 Combats and their outcomes

Count up the number of "fighting stands" in a unit. (see diagram).

COMBAT

ROMANS

1	2	3	4	5	6

A	B		D		
F	G	C	I	E	
		H		J	

BRITONS

The Romans have 3 stands in contact with the enemy (1, 2 and 4) so 2 outflanking an enemy stand (3 and 5) so they roll 5 Combat dice. 6 is not involved in this combat

The British warband is 10 stands strong, in two ranks, but stands C and E were stopped short by Roman pila, holding up the stands behind (H and J). This leaves the Britons with 3 stands in contact (A, B and D). Half the stands behind them also count, so that's one more stand (1½ rounds down to one), so they roll a total of 4 Combat dice.

The fighting stands are:
a) Any stands which are touching and facing an enemy stand to their front or are outflanking one. A stand which is defending fortifications cannot be outflanked.
b) Half of any second rank stands who are behind a fighting first rank stand and facing the same way. Don't count any second rank stands in the case of Infantry who are fighting over fortifications or Cavalry who are attacking the front of formed infantry.

For each fighting stand roll one Combat Dice. Roll only half the dice if the unit is disordered.

In the **first turn** of a combat Archers & Slingers need to roll a 6 to score a hit, Skirmishers and Chariots need 5/6 and all other troops need 4/5/6. Warbands & Heavy Cavalry hit for 3/4/5/6 when they are charging an enemy in the open.

In a second or later turn of combat between the same opponents, Legionaries still need 4/5/6, to hit, Archers, Slingers, Chariots & Skirmishers need a 6, and all other troops need 5/6.

Make saving throws for any hits suffered (as in 1.3, above). The side that takes the most stands destroyed in the fighting is the loser. If both sides lose the same number of stands, Roman Legionaries and Auxilia count as the winners. Otherwise the two sides remain locked in combat.

The loser of any turn of fighting must back off 8cm in its current formation – ie keeping any gaps or irregularities in its line that were caused by the fighting. The Combat will only continue next turn if either side chooses to attack and renew the combat any stands that back off into friends are disordered or **destroyed** if they back off into enemies. Britons who back off into woods keep going for one full move.

3.3 Close Ranks after Combat

Roman Legionaries and **Auxilia** always close their ranks at the end of a round of combat, by moving all the stands in a unit back together to fill any gaps caused by the fighting.

Other troops can only do this as part of a "re-group" action (see 2.3(c) above) in the next turn.

3.4 Special cases

Artillery which is attacked is always overrun and destroyed without rolling any Combat dice (the crew abandon these weapons before the enemy get to close quarters).

Elephants that fail a saving throw or that are on the losing side in a round of combat always turn around and run straight back for one move, fighting an extra round of combat against anyone in their way (even against friendly troops!) before bursting through and running off the battlefield, trumpeting …

So why did anybody bother using such unpredictable beasts? Their main effect was as a "terror weapon" – horses who were unfamiliar with their smell wouldn't go anywhere near them! So, in this game, **British Cavalry or Chariots are not allowed to move within 16cm of an Elephant**.

Phase 4: Unit Morale and Discipline

4.1 Morale

Any units which have lost half of their original number of stands cannot attack.

Units which have lost **more than half** of their original stands react in different ways:
a) **Legionaries** and **Auxilia** must **withdraw**, facing the enemy, until they can move behind a friendly unit. While doing this Legionaries may lock their shields (show this by replacing one of the stands with a "testudo" model) – if attacked they minus 1 on their Combat dice (so hit only for 5/6) but add 1 to saving throws (so save for 2/3/4/5/6)
b) **Skirmishers** and **Missile troops** are put **out of action** – remove any remaining stands from the battlefield, keeping them separate from the army's "dead pool".
c) **Other troops Rout.** They turn their backs (this takes half a move) and then flee the battlefield. They will always run back over their home edge of the battlefield by the shortest route, avoiding any enemy units but running through any friends who are in their way – this may start a Panic. If attacked while fleeing they get no Combat dice and all fleeing troops need a 6 for a saving throw.

4.2 Panic

If a unit has friends flee through it, or sees friends fleeing past within 12cm it must immediately test to see if this sets off a panic. Roll a D6. It must score higher than the current number of stands lost by the unit, otherwise the unit panics and joins the runaways.

Britons always minus 1 from the dice roll.

Roman Legionaries and Auxilia always add 1 (they know there is nowhere safe to run to …!).

4.3 Pursuit

Warbands whose enemy run away after Combat always pursue them until they are destroyed. Cavalry test for pursuit. Roll a D6: Britons always -1, Romans -1 or +1, at their player's choice.

Pursue for a score of 3 or less with the pursuit lasting for the

dice rolled x turns - *put the dice beside the two mixed-up units to remind you how long it will last* - before the pursuers stop and can try to rally. If the pursuit takes them off the battlefield they never come back. Pursued troops keep running and never rally. Troops who are attacked while pursuing count disordered.

Phase 5. Re-forming from Disorder and Rallying

The last action at the end of a turn is that any units:-

a) Which were disordered during the turn as a result of crossing an obstacle or as a result of being "passed through" by friendly troops can now re-form their ranks, on the spot.

b) Which have ceased pursuing a fleeing enemy roll a D6. (Romans +1). Rally and Reform the ranks for 4/5/6, otherwise spend the next turn in disorder, then roll again.

Phase 6: Victory and Defeat

An army is defeated when its Commanders or its troops (or both!) lose heart and decide to call it a day. In our games, we usually expect a gentlemanly Player to recognise when it is time to concede gracefully. But we also have a rule that the moment of victory or defeat comes:

a) When one Army achieves any special victory conditions set out before the battle, OR

b) When a British Army's Commander is killed or leaves the battlefield, OR

c) When an army that has already crossed its agreed Breaking Point (see Setting up the Battle) has one of its units routed, panicked or forced to withdraw (see Phase 4). This event sets off a general collapse in the army's morale.

Destroyed, routed and panicked stands count their full points lost. Missile troops or Skirmishers who are merely put out of action – see 4.1(b) – don't count towards losses.

A player can ask for a "points count" of both armies' losses at the end of any turn.

COMMAND AND CONTROL

Leaders (Roman "Generals" and British Chiefs) have an important role to play in encouraging their troops (*although leading a unit into action can be a risky business!*).

Each army should have approximately one Leader for every six units in the army (not counting skirmishers or slingers). One leader represents you as the Army Commander.

Roman leaders are mounted and can move up to 40cm to join any unit. They always move first, then can move again with the unit they have joined.

British chiefs always join a Bodyguard unit (Cavalry or Warband) at the start of a battle and then must stay with it until the end. Put them behind the unit's front rank

If a leader has joined a unit he may re-roll one of its dice, **once per turn**, for any purpose, such as Orders, Shooting, Combat, Saving or Rallying.

If a unit a leader has joined ever loses a stand in a round of Combat roll 2D6 (*with no re-roll!*):

2 = the Leader is killed,

3 or 4 = he is wounded, so he can't do any more re-rolls.

If he gets a second wound he has to leave the battlefield.

If a British chief is killed or takes two wounds his Bodyguard unit will disengage and carry him off the battlefield. Romans just carry on fighting if anything happens to any of their Leaders...

Druids are a special sort of British Leader. They don't command units in battle – instead they encourage the warriors by convincing them that their magical powers will give protection from enemy weapons. At the start of a battle a British army with a druid can upgrade one Warband from "aggressive" to "fanatical" – the unit will re-roll (once) any failed Combat throws the first time it attacks and any failed saving throws the first time it takes any hits. During the battle Druids remain behind the lines, casting spells and sacrificing ...

GAME PLAY AND TACTICS

Both sides need to weigh up their tactical options on each turn depending on if they get to shoot or move first. This can tip the advantage one way or the other.

After the initial shock, infantry combats can be hard slogs and shooting is largely indecisive. But battle casualties can mount up alarmingly fast if one side tries to break off and run away.

Britons will soon find that the Romans tend to have the edge in a stand up fight, so will do best to try and wear them down first by skulking in ambush and launching tip and run attacks with Chariots, Cavalry and Skirmishers. The Warbands are always going to be hard to control and liable to attack without orders, but their initial charge can be very effective if the dice gods are with them!

Romans need to exercise a careful and patient approach coupled with ruthless aggression whenever the opportunity presents itself. The Legionaries are the toughest troops on the battlefield but other Romans are more evenly matched by their British equivalents. The Britons are tricky and dangerous opponents, so they should never be underestimated. Their weakness is that they lack discipline, so they are liable to make rash attacks or panic in adversity.

SOME FINAL WORDS

These rules can't cover every possible situation that might emerge in a game. In such cases the only way to avoid argument and decide a point at issue is to boil it down to a question of "Can you do something, Yes or No?" roll dice to decide, then move on with the game. You can discuss it at greater length afterwards and perhaps agree a "house rule" for future use. Most wargames rules evolve in this way. And if you really don't like a rule, feel free to change it!

Many rule writers seek to avoid this sort of thing by trying to explain everything in minute detail and at great length. These days it is commonplace for published wargames rules to run to over a hundred pages of text.

We didn't have the space or inclination to do this here. Our experience shows anyway that the more you try to tighten up rules, the more legalistic they become, often to no good purpose.

ROMANS vs BRITONS: PLAYSHEET

All moves are in multiples of 8cms/3 inches/ 2 stand widths. Ranges are in multiples of 4cms.
Dice = D6. Halves always round DOWN.

TROOP TYPES AND STATISTICS

Troops (points)	Move / Change	Shooting Dice per stand	Range cms	Saving Throw	Notes
Legionaries (2)	16	1 (pila)	8	3/4/5/6	Close ranks. Testudo
Auxilia (2)	24	1 (javelins)	8	4/5/6	Close ranks
Archers (2)	16	2	24	5/6	{ May shoot ½ & move ½
Slingers (1)	24	1	24	5/6	{ 6 to hit in Combat
Warbands* (2)	16/24	0		4/5/6	Charge
Skirmishers (1)	24	1	8	5/6	6 to hit in combat
Light Cavalry* (2)	32	1	8	5/6	May evade charge
Heavy Cavalry* (2)	32/40	0		4/5/6	Charge
Chariots (2)	32	1	8	4/5/6	Act independently
Artillery (2)	8	2	32	5/6	Overrun in combat
Elephants (2)	16	0		3/4/5/6	No enemy Horses within 16cm
Leader (n/a)	Roman 40* Briton as Bodyguard unit*	n/a	n/a	n/a	Unit gets a re-roll

TURN SEQUENCE

1. Shooting (Archers, Artillery & Slingers)
2. Movement (including throwing any Javelins by Light Cavalry, Chariots & Skirmishers)
3. Close Combat (including throwing any Pila or Javelins by Legionaries and Auxilia)
4. Morale
5. Rallying

ORGANISATION

Infantry: Usually 6 stands per unit but Warbands can be 6, 8 or 10 stands strong.

Cavalry: 6 stands per unit

Artillery & Elephants: 3 stands per unit. Single stands may be attached to Infantry units.

Chariots: Single stands which act independently. They may also join a friendly unit for Combat.

SHOOTING

Dice each turn for who shoots first (Britons win a tie)

1D6 per stand (2D6 Artillery & Archers). ½ dice vs skirmishers/slingers/chariots. Hit for 6

Archers & Slingers: May roll ½ dice and then move ½ distance.

Javelins: Throw before/during/after movement. 6s hit. Saving throws for hits on Miss/Sk/LCav/Char.

Other targets are driven back 4cm (1 base depth), disrupting their formation (as for "Pila").

Pila (Legionaries) and Javelins (Auxilia): See Combat.

SAVING THROWS

If a unit takes hits Roll 1 dice: count that number from right (even)/left (odd) to see which stand is hit.

Roll a dice for each hit (+1 in fortifications or testudo). See "Saving Throws" listed by troop Type.

A failed throw means the stand is destroyed. Keep count of points lost.

MOVEMENT

Dice each turn to see who moves first (Romans win a tie). Make any compulsory moves first.

Orders: Roll 1 dice per unit or per group of Roman units, to do anything within 32cms of enemy.

British Warbands and Heavy Cavalry: 1 or 2 must attack.

Other Troops: 1 = ½ speed or no special manoeuvre.

No need to roll if British Heavy Cavalry or Warband who are ordered to advance.

British Chariots always act independently on their own initiative so never need to roll.

A **Normal move** is straight ahead or forward diagonally up to 45 degrees right/left.

Infantry can also back off half a move, facing the enemy.

Charges (Warbands & Hvy Cavalry) must be in a straight line: enemy must be at least ½ move away.

SPECIAL MOVES AND MANOUEVRES

Re-group: Romans can re-arrange the stands in a unit in any way, then make a half move.

Britons can re-arrange a dice x stands in a unit (treat this as their Orders dice) and then make a half move.

Wheeling is by pivoting on one end of the line.

Legionaries, Warbands, Archers & Elephants: wheel up to 90 degrees on the spot, or up to 45 degrees and then make a half move.

Auxilia & Cavalry can wheel up to 90 degrees and then move or vice versa.

Skirmishers, Slingers and Chariots can wheel and move in any way, up to their maximum moves.

About Face: all troops except chariots and Skirmishers take half a move.

Taking Ground is by edging sideways at half speed.

Passing Through: Romans can pass through any stationary friends.

Passing Through: Britons must roll a dice, needing 4/5/6, else both units are temporarily disordered

Obstacles Legionaries, Warbands and Mounted Troops are temporarily disordered when crossing them – halt on the other side (disordered) for the rest of the turn. Other troops are not affected.

COMBAT

Legionaries throw **pila** just before combat, Roll 1 dice per front rank stand for the 1st round, then half the front rank for the 2nd.

6s to hit. Auxilia throw javelins, half the front rank in the 1st or 2nd round

Any Defenders stands who are hit are driven back 4cm, Attackers will stop 4cm short

Count up the number of "fighting stands" = stands in contact or outflanking an enemy stand, plus half of the second rank (n/a Cav vs formed Inf or Inf behind fortifications) who are behind "fighting stands"

Count only half this total number of stands if the unit is disordered. Roll the final total x dice.

1st round: Hit for 4/5/6, Skirmishers & Chariots 5/6, Missile troops 6. Charging WB/H.Cav. re-roll 1s

2nd and later rounds: Legionaries hit for 4/5/6, Missile troops, Skirmishers & Chariots for 6, all others for 5/6

Make saving throws for any hits, as under Shooting. The loser must fall back 8cms. Legionaries & Auxilia win any draws and re-group after combat.

——— MORALE ———

Losses: After losing half its strength a unit cannot attack after losing more than half its strength:

Legionaries and Auxilia must **Withdraw**, facing the enemy (Legionaries may lock shields in "testudo")

Skirmishers & missile troops are put **Out of Action** – remove any remaining stands.

Other troops **Rout** = turn around (takes ½ move) and flee the battlefield. They get no Combat dice if attacked while fleeing. Infantry -2 on saving throws, Cavalry & Chariots -1.

Pursuit: Victorious Warbands always pursue a fleeing enemy. Cavalry test to see if they pursue.

Roll a dice: Britons -1, Romans can choose +1 or -1. Pursue for a final score of 3 or less

The pursuit lasts for the dice rolled x moves. Pursuers count disordered if attacked.

Panic:

Test immediately if a unit has friends run away through it or sees them running past within 12cm.

Roll a dice and score more than the current number of stands lost by the unit, else it joins the rout.

Britons always -1, Legionaries & Auxilia +1.

—— RE-FORMING FROM DISORDER AND RALLYING ——

At the end of a turn any troops that were disordered during the turn as a result of a crossing an obstacle, or by being "passed through", can now rally automatically. Test to rally at the end of a pursuit. Roll a dice (Romans +1). Re-form for 4/5/6.

——— LEADERS ———

If attached to a unit he may re-roll one of its dice (for any purpose) in a turn.

If the unit ever loses at least one stand in combat roll 2 dice :-

2 = The Leader is Killed. A British army is defeated at the moment its Commander is killed.

3 or 4 = He is wounded - out of action for this turn & the next. Leave the battlefield after 2 wounds.

——— VICTORY AND DEFEAT ———

Once its Breaking Point is crossed, an Army is defeated the next time one of its units panics, routs or withdraws. Destroyed, Fleeing and Panicked stands count their full points lost.

Ignore any Skirmishers and Slingers who were merely put "out of action" (Rule 4.1b).

A British army is also defeated at the moment its Commander is killed or leaves the battlefield.

BATTLES FOR BRITANNIA

Here are three battle scenarios for you to try out, loosely based on historical events and in ascending order of complexity. The silly names are optional, of course, but this sort of thing is traditional amongst wargamers of a certain age and immaturity…

1. AMBUSH

A small Roman army is marching to the relief of a beleaguered northern fort.

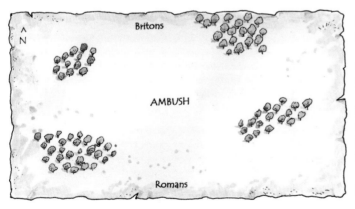

unit enters the wood). The other units can be deployed anywhere north of a line between the two southern woods.

Objective: to prevent the enemy marching off the northern edge of the battlefield.

Roman Army

Commander: Tribune Gluteus Maximus

2 units of Legionaries, 2 of Auxilia, 1 of Heavy Cavalry, 1 of Skirmishers. (66 points, Breaking point 22).

Units enter the battlefield two at a time, anywhere on the southern edge.

Objective: To march off the northern edge of the battlefield before the army's breaking point has been crossed

British Army

Commander: Cumulonimbus, war chief of the Canelloni.

3 Warbands (2 @ 8 stands, 1 @ 6), 1 unit of Light Cavalry, 2 of Slingers, 1 of Skirmishers and 5 stands of Chariots. (84 points, Breaking point 28).

Warbands can start the battle hidden in the trees – no more than one warband to each patch of woods (use markers, including a dummy and don't reveal them until they leave cover or a Roman

2. WARRIOR QUEEN

Make or break for the great British rebellion.
This game is probably best with two players a side.

British Army

Commanders: Verucca, Warrior Queen of the Alumni & Stratocumulus, her War Chief

6 Warbands (2 @ 10 stands, 2 @ 8 and 2 @ 6), 1 unit of Heavy Cavalry, 1 of Light Cavalry, 2 of Slingers, 1 of Skirmishers and 6 stands of Chariots. (150 points, breaking point 50).

Deploy anywhere north of the stream. One unit may be concealed in each of the woods – these are your encampments and both of them have felled trees and other improvised defences around their perimeter.

Objective: to defeat the Roman army and capture their Marching Fort.

Special Rule

The Queen does not join in the fighting, but any unit within 12cms of her can re-roll one of its dice in any turn.

Roman Army

Commanders: Legate Bibulus Forex and Tribune Lucius Lasticus.
3 units of Legionaries, 3 of Auxilia, 1 of Light Cavalry, 1 of Archers, 2 of Skirmishers and 3 stands of Artillery. (114 points, Breaking Point 38).

Deploy anywhere south of the stream, including behind the ramparts of the Marching Fort.

Objective: to defeat the British army and capture one of their woodland encampments.

3. AMPHIBIOUS ASSAULT

D-Day for the Romans and the Druids' last stand.

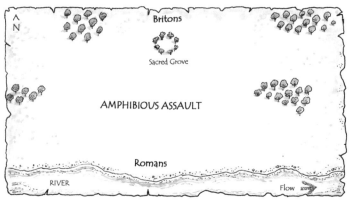

British Army

Commander: Abracadabrus (Chief Druid).

6 Warbands (2 @ 10 stands, 2 @ 8 and 2 @ 6), 4 units of Slingers and 8 stands of Chariots (136 points, breaking point 46).

Roll a dice at the start of the game to upgrade the roll x Warbands to "fanatical" status.

Deploy anywhere on the northern half of the map, including one unit hidden in each wood (if you wish).

Objective: to repel the Roman invaders from the sacred shores of Cardamon.

Roman Army

Commander: Legate Dubious Asparagus.

4 units of Legionaries, 3 of Auxilia, 1 of Skirmishers, 1 of Heavy Cavalry, 1 of Archers and 3 stands of Artillery. (120 points, Breaking Point 40).

The army's starting position is off the southern end of the battlefield and it has to cross a river estuary at dawn to get at the enemy's sacred stronghold on the island of Cardamon.

You will have to do this by making an amphibious assault crossing – a dangerous operation! You have 6 boats available and each boat can hold three stands of infantry (of any type). You can also fit a Scorpion in the sterncastle, if you trim its base.

Your boats can land at any point on the north shore of the river. To cross the water you must roll a dice for each boat at the start of your Movement phase: 4/5/6 it succeeds and the troops disembark. Re-cross next turn to pick up another load. 2/3 it only gets half way across – try to land again next turn 1 it fails and the strong current sends it downstream 12 cms. Try again next turn. Boats can't move upstream - only across stream or downstream. But they can also just hold their position offshore – which is useful for archers or artillery to lay down covering fire.

Any boat that goes off the eastern edge is swept further downstream and can't return.

In addition, you have sent your Cavalry and Skirmishers off to try and find somewhere to swim across and outflank the enemy position (they are Batavian Cohors Equitata, particularly skilled at such operations). Roll a dice at the beginning of each turn and, on a roll of 6, they appear on either the eastern or western edge of the battlefield (you chose which). The Cavalry can also operate on foot (as Auxilia) – it takes half a turn for them to dismount.

Objective: to defeat the British army and capture the Sacred Grove.

Special rules

If the Romans capture the Sacred Grove and set fire to it all British units must take a Panic Test. A Roman unit must be in sole occupation of the grove without any fighting in it for a whole turn in order to achieve this. Roman Legionaries and Auxilia who are defeated in combat cannot be forced back into the river – they will fight to the death at the water's edge instead.

ROMANS vs BRITONS: RULES FOR ABSOLUTE BEGINNERS

Make two armies

The Roman army has five units (2 Legionaries, 1 Auxilia, 1 Archers and 1 Cavalry), each of 6 stands.

A total army strength of 30 stands plus one mounted General. The British army has four Warbands (2 of 8 stands and 2 of 6 stands), one unit of Slingers (6 stands) and one unit of Cavalry (6 stands). A total army strength of 40 stands plus one Chief in a Chariot

Set up the two armies, facing each other and 60 cm apart. See the diagram below for a typical starting line-up. Each unit should have all its stands arranged in a single rank, touching each other.

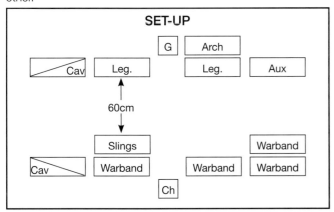

Ready to start?

The game is played as a series of turns. Each turn has 4 stages that must be played through in this order every time: 1. Shoot, 2. Move, 3. Fight, 4. Discipline.

Stage 1: Shoot

Both Players roll a dice. The one with the highest score shoots first. Britons win a tie.

How far? The range for Archers and Slingers is 24cm. **If no targets are in range move on to Stage 2.**

Who can I shoot at? Choose your target from any enemy troops who are in range of any of your Archers or Slingers and not involved in a fight. You can't target the enemy Commander! Archers can shoot over the heads of friendly troops if the target is over half range.

What's the damage? Roll 1 dice for every stand shooting. Any 6s you get are hits. Troops who are hit must then make a Saving Throw. The Player who is shooting decides which enemy stands are hit.

Legionaries: save for 3,4,5,6. A roll of 1 or 2 means the stand is destroyed – take it off the table.

Auxilia, Warbands and Cavalry: save for 4,5,6, destroyed for 1,2,3

Slingers and Archers: save for 5,6, destroyed for 1,2,3,4

Stage 2: Move

Both sides roll a dice. The Player with the highest score moves first. Romans win a tie

Who can move? Any unit which didn't shoot this turn.

How far? Legionaries, Archers and Warbands: 16cm. Warbands can "Charge" 24cm to contact the enemy.

Auxilia and Slingers: 24 cm

Cavalry and Commanders: 32 cm. Cavalry can charge 40cm to contact the enemy.

These are maximum move rates for movement straight ahead, although a little "drift" is OK.

To charge, you MUST move straight ahead and the enemy must be at least half a charge move away.

You can move only half this distance if you change direction with a unit of Legionaries or Warband or Archers, or if you re-arrange the stands in any unit before you move it.

Roman units can move through each other. British Slingers can move through any other British units. If Warbands or Cavalry try to do this roll a dice – if the score is 1,2 or 3 the two units get mixed up and fail to complete the manoeuvre. They can't re-arrange themselves until the next turn.

Any move that brings a unit into contact with the enemy becomes an Attack and leads to a Fight.

Stage 3: Fight

Work out the fights between units one at a time.

Roman Legionaries and Auxilia use their heavy throwing spears just before a fight starts. Roll one dice for each stand involved in the combat. Any 6s are hits. Roll a saving dice for every hit, just like in shooting. Each unit can only throw these weapons once in a battle.

Who can fight? Count up all the stands that are touching or outflanking an enemy stand (see diagram) and then roll that many Combat Dice.

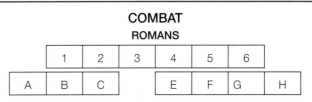

The Romans have 5 stands in contact with the enemy (1,2,4,5 & 6) and one outflanking (3) so they roll a total of six Combat dice.

British stand "D" was destroyed when the Romans threw their pila, so the Britons have 5 stands in contact (B,C,E,F & G) and 2 stands outflanking (A & H), so they roll a total of seven Combat dice.

Legionaries hit for 4,5,6 Auxilia, Cavalry & Warbands hit for 5 or 6, Slingers & Archers hit only for 6.

Warbands and Cavalry who are charging hit for 3/4/5/6. A Warband can only charge once in the battle, a Cavalry unit can charge twice.

Make a saving throw for every hit.

Who wins? The side that lost the most stands in a fight is the loser. Romans win if it is a draw. The losing side must back off 8cm. Renew the fight next turn if either side attacks again.

Stage 4: Discipline

At the end of a round of fighting Roman Legionaries and Auxilia use their superb training to re-arrange their stands and close any gaps made in their lines by losses. Other Romans and all British troops can only do this at the start of their next move, and then can only move half distance.

Any unit that has lost half of its stands cannot attack but it can still defend itself.

Any unit that has lost more than half of its stands must retreat. Roman Legionaries and Auxilia do this by backing off, facing the enemy, at 8cm a turn, until they can take shelter behind a friendly unit. If attacked they will defend themselves to the last stand.

All other units must turn and run away straight back to their own table edge, by the shortest route. Runaways are always the first units you move at the start of the next Move stage. They avoid any enemy troops but will run through any friendly troops in their way. If a unit has friends run through it or running past within 12cm it must take a Panic Test. Ignore any runaway Slingers or Archers.

Panic Test: Roll a dice. Add 1 if the unit testing is Roman. Minus 1 for each stand already lost by the unit that is testing. If the final score is 1 or less the unit panics and joins the mob of runaways.

Commanders

A Roman General or British Chief represents you, as the Army Commander.

You can move the Commander to join a unit (put him behind the front rank). This gives you the right to re-roll one of the dice rolled by that unit during the rest of the turn. This might be any of the dice rolled for Shooting or Fighting or Saving or for a Panic Test. But if the unit you are leading loses one or more stands in Fighting (not from Shooting) you are at risk. Roll 2 dice (you can't re-roll these!). If the score is 2 or 3 the Commander has been killed in action! All British units must take an immediate panic test if their Chief is killed. Romans simply ignore the loss of their General and carry on fighting.

So who wins the battle?

Count the number of stands lost (destroyed or running away) by each side at the end of every turn.

If one army has lost more than half of the number of stands it started with, then it has lost the battle. If both armies have lost more than half then it is a draw. Time to schedule a re-match!

Further reading

There are lots of books on the Roman army and its wars against the Britons, but anyone writing about this must draw heavily on two ancient authors, namely Caesar (The Gallic Wars books IV and V) and Tacitus (The Agricola and Annals Books XII and XIV). Translations of all these are readily available online or in cheap paperback editions, so you might as well start your reading with the original sources.

Of more recent books, Osprey Publishing have this period well covered – numbers 46 and 158 in their Men-at-Arms series describe the Roman and British armies, respectively and number 233 in the Campaign series gives a full account of Boudicca's Rebellion (incidentally, with illustrations by Peter). Warlord Games' "Britannia", a supplement for the popular "Hail Caesar" rules, gives comprehensive coverage of the Roman conquest of this new province and its potential as a subject for wargaming.

The Romans have exhausted the land by their indiscriminate plunder. To robbery, butchery and rapine they give the lying name of "government"; they create a desolation and call it peace. Their army is a motley conglomeration of nations. See them, a scanty band, scared and bewildered, staring blankly at the sky, sea and forests around them. And beyond this army that you see there is nothing to be afraid of – only forts without garrisons, colonies of greybeards, towns sick and distracted between rebel subjects and tyrant masters. On then, into action! The gods will grant us the vengeance we deserve! The Romans will never face even the din and roar of all our thousands, much less the shock of our onslaught. Consider how many of you are fighting and let us show, at the very first clash of arms, what manner of men we are! Today will mean the dawn of liberty for the whole of Britain.
(King Calgacus)

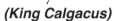

The enemy are coming now, for we have dug them out of their hiding places. The long road that we have travelled, the forests we have threaded our way through, the estuaries we have crossed – all will be to our credit and honour as long as we keep our eyes to the front. We have not the exact knowledge of the country that our enemy has, but we have our hands, with swords in them, and these are all that matters. Disregard the clamour and empty threats of the barbarians. In their ranks, there are more women than fighting men. Unwarlike, lacking armour, when they see the arms and courage of the conquerors who have routed them so often, they will break immediately. Just keep in close order. Throw your javelins, and then carry on : use your shield bosses to fell them, swords to kill them. Do not think of plunder. When you have won, you will have everything.
(Gnaeus Julius Agricola)